Preaching with Fire

Dr. Daniel Kazemian

NEW HARBOR PRESS
RAPID CITY, SD

Copyright © 2020 by Daniel Kazemian.

All rights reserved. No part of this publication may be reproduced, distributed or transmitted in any form or by any means, including photocopying, recording, or other electronic or mechanical methods, without the prior written permission of the publisher, except in the case of brief quotations embodied in critical reviews and certain other noncommercial uses permitted by copyright law. For permission requests, write to the publisher, addressed "Attention: Permissions Coordinator," at the address below.

Kazemian/New Harbor Press
1601 Mt. Rushmore Rd., Ste 3288
Rapid City, SD 57701
www.NewHarborPress.com

Ordering Information:
Quantity sales. Special discounts are available on quantity purchases by corporations, associations, and others. For details, contact the "Special Sales Department" at the address above.

Preaching with Fire/Daniel Kazemian. -- 1st ed.

ISBN 978-1-63357-341-3

Contents

Introduction 1

Preaching of Noah 7

The Ministry of Abraham 19

The Life of Joseph 29

The Mission of Moses 39

The Courage of Joshua 51

The Twelve Judges 63

God Sent Fire from Heaven 77

The Holy Spirit like a Fire 101

Baptism in the Holy Spirit 123

Speaking in Tongues 137

The Fire of God and Prayer 149

Relationship with the Fire 155

Jesus Calls Us to the Ministry 175

How I received the Fire of God 183

How to become a Christian? 199

Conclusion 203
About the Author 207

Introduction

WE WILL LOOK AT how we can preach with the fire of the Holy Spirit. Where is the Fire? Is the fire still burning in all churches? Can we have the Fire in all denominations today? Why there are some Christians Fellowship will have a powerful Fire and but in other congregations can be found a small Fire?

There are many questions we can ask in this book! I will answer all questions, and we will learn how to get our Fire burning all the time in our hearts. Preaching of His Word that brings fresh anointing of the Holy Spirit in the Church.

We received a great promise of the outpouring of His Fire come on us. That' why we can stand firm in His Might to speak the Word of God. What the Bible defines God is as "a consuming fire."

We have seen what the presence of the Lord made the fire to consume the burnt offering on the altar. In fact, God lighted the Fire on Alter by Himself. It presented the fire as a holy gift offering.

I will be using the word: "Fire" in this book many times and many places. Because my focus is to make sure that we understand how we can preach the Word with Fire? So, it is a surprise that there are two kinds of fire often presents in the Old Testament sacrifices. One natural fire and another one is a divine fire as a manifestation of God's presence and God's Glory.

We will be focusing on a few servants of the Lord in the Bible, how to stay strong to preach the Gospel. The Word said we must be a witness by the power of the Holy Spirit. We will get into many illustrations about Fire.

We search about how those men, like kings, prophets, judges, and servants of God, they had experience with the presence of God. Fire in the Bible will present a great action of the Holy Spirit. The presence of God is always trying to live in the believer's heart. The Holy Spirit came down for His Churches in the New Testament.

The Spirit is manifesting himself with a fire at least three forms or more. He draws God's presence to His people in the temple. He comes down with His Glory in the Tabernacles of meeting in the Old Testament.

Later on, we will learn about God's passion and God's purity. We see, in the New Covenant, John Baptist predicted that the One would come after me. He shall baptize us with the Holy Spirit and the Fire.

At the very beginning of Christianity, they followed the Holy Spirit with fire. When the Holy Spirit brought the Fire for a new outpouring at Pentecost day in the early church. He appeared as "tongues of fire" breathing on each disciple.

All disciples and followers of Jesus were ready to receive the empowerment of the Spirit of God. There was a great promise from Jesus has been fulfilled that they needed more power and more Fire to preach the Good News with no fear.

They all were waiting to get filled with the Holy Spirit. Suddenly the presence of the Holy Spirit brought a mighty wind of fire as a new glory pouring down from heaven with a new language. They received a fresh visitation from the Living Spirit to speak in other tongues as the Spirit has empowered them.

When we study the New Testament, we acknowledged how the Lord directs His followers to get encouraged in the Fire and to become active in the Word. As we know, the Holy Spirit dwells in our souls, and we received a new spirit. He made us a new "temple of the Spirit of the living God."

The Holy Spirit is pouring out the joy of the Lord in our hearts. After Jesus resurrected, He met the two traveling followers who spoke with Him on the road. They expressed themselves with fantastic courage in their hearts as they said, "burning within us."

All apostles were, along with other disciples of Jesus, have received new empowerment of the Fire of God on the Day of Pentecost. They had a zeal to preach with the Fire and to preach the message of Salvation boldly.

The Holy Spirit carries out the purity of God for us, as always, God's will is to purify His saints. The Spirit wants to sanctify us by His Word and

His blood. His fire would have to cleanse and remove impurities. We always remember the Fire is from the presence of the Holy Spirit.

The Fire is God's glory to be released into the hungry man and woman of God. When someone is asking more of God, more of His anointing. Then the Fire will be sent out into every heart to become equipped into glorious preaching.

The Fire of God is an anointing of His Presence and His Glory, which has operated several times in the Old Testament. ***The Fire of God*** would represent which in several events: God's Glory, God's power, God's wrath, God's Holiness, God's judgment has demonstrated from heaven.

• CHAPTER 1 •

Preaching of Noah

I WANT TO START from the Old Testament, in which we read stories from those men who were walking with God. They had the heart to listen to what God had a plan for them. There cannot be found any name of the preacher in the Old Testament.

There were all servants of God, such as *priests* serving in the temple. God appointed *kings* to reign over the people. God elected *judges* to rule over the nation. God has chosen *prophets* to deliver the messages of God.

Some men were preaching with passion, and there was no compromise with any other gods around them. These men were preaching with the Fire, and let's look at Noah's desire to do the work of God. Noah was following with a plan that what he had in his heart.

He had favor with God and acceptance in the eyes of the Lord. Noah had a love for God and a heart for the lost people. Noah had great faith in God, and he was indeed a righteous man.

The Bible tells us; the name of Noah means in Hebrew: 'rest' or 'comfort' from all the significant attempts a fellow man comes to experience in the tragedy in the Garden of Eden. As we know, the 'curse' has started from the disobedience of Adam and Eve.

God allowed Noah to reach out to many could to repent their sins. He received an authority to carry out a significant task to serve God's plan. He instructed Noah to lead into new adventures to build up a massive ark for his generations.

This plan involved wiping humankind off the face of the earth. At the age of 480, he had been carrying a heart with Fire in the spirit of God. He devoted his desire steadily into a life of obedience.

Nevertheless, he may also have been frightened by such a massive plan. God directed Noah to build an ark for 120 years. He was giving people plenty of time to repent and turn from their evil ways. It took a long time to finish the Ark.

Finally, God sends a heavy rain down to earth for 40 days non-stop. There was very heavy rain, and the water covered the whole ground. No one could escape from the massive flood.

It is believed three billion people perished in that flood, and only eight people survived—those in Noah's family and along with their animals, livestock who were safe on the ark. After the flood, God promised Noah that humans would never be wiped out again through the flood.

God established the rainbow as a sign that He would keep his word throughout all the generations to come. After the flood, Noah lived 350 years, and he died at the age of 950. God began to bless Noah and his sons.

God granted them to rule over every creature that runs on the ground. Over every fowl flying through the air and, overall, the fishes of the sea. Every livestock on ground moves shall be meat for them to eat, alike as the fresh herb.

He told them to be fruitful and restore your life and the earth. He will deliver them all to you. The first action of Noah after getting off the ark was to set up an altar before the Almighty God. He gives an offering of sacrifice in gratitude.

We recognize from scripture that the first altar has been placed in the book of Genesis. Noah gave an offering of every pure beast and fowl that they had been with him in the ark. God decided to provide salvation possible for Noah since he could not save himself without grace.

Imagine if Noah wanted to follow his own plan rather than God's way? He couldn't succeed. God directed Noah through the whole disaster flood, despite all the taunts and mockery. But God was in complete authority over His plan to finish humanity. Noah's faith had saved him by grace through obedience to God, he preached with a passion, but no one could believe in him.

But Noah knew there must be a reason God told him to build an ark. It may Noah preached to himself, and he encouraged himself about the salvation of God. If we are given a message to preach and if we make the same choice to obey and follow Him today.

We, as Christians, have learned many great messages from Noah. Those people were living with no faith in God. There was no desire for them to believe anything else except believing themselves.

At the same people we have here today, there are millions of people who are around us. Some people believe in God; some believe nothing. Some are believing in their own God or trusting in their own religion.

Noah Warned Them:
Noah wanted to warn them; there will be a disaster with the judgment of God will come down from heaven. We cannot find any verse in the book of Genesis said that he was preaching.

But there is research that will confirm that he shared his wonderful testimony on His preaching to the people in which they didn't care about God. These are the evidence of his generations.

He had many challenges to deal with many non-believers. In the time of his life and he was living among wicked people. They were all living with an evil lifestyle surrendered him with all non-sense thoughts. But none of them had any sense of awareness of God.

He was the first evangelist revealed in the Bible. Are there any messages of his way of life that can prepare us about how to preach the truth with the glorious Fire of God's presence?

Whatever, Noah had significantly encountered God and with His plan, which he received to speak the Word and to do what it needs to be done. We probably have the same events as we Christians run into confronting the message of salvation today.

Corrupted People:
Where the people are filled with an evil mind, and it will turn into the wrong action. When the heart of every man became callous, and careless not pay attention to the way of God. The devil comes to destroy lives every day.

When we study the Word in the time of Noah said; the whole earth became corrupted. The people were thoughtless; then, the Lord did not have any tolerance; it reached up into the sight of God, and they overflowed the earth with ruthlessness.

Therefore, later between Noah's age from 500 to 600 years, God instructed Noah He made the final decision to wipe out humanity with a flood. He ordered him to make an ark, so he and his household would be protected through it, as **"But I will establish My covenant with you; and you shall go into the ark—you, your sons, your wife, and your sons' wives with you."** Genesis 6:18, NKJV.

Noah could have preached with the Fire of God anywhere near 100 years about the coming God's judgment. Some believe God was reducing man's lifetime, the length of time for which a person to 120 years. But there's no actual or scriptural evidence to support that.

The text of Genesis 6 is punishment so, and it's very further possible that God was giving humankind 120 years before wiping them out.

And the Lord said, **"My Spirit shall not strive with man forever, for he is indeed flesh; yet his days shall be one hundred and twenty years."** Genesis 6:3, NKJV.

In the book of Genesis indicates the flood rise when Noah was 600 years old.

"Noah was six hundred years old when the floodwaters were on the earth." Genesis 7:6, NKJV.

Faith in Noah:
Let's continue to look at the most profound faith of Noah. God has revealed Himself to him, and God put faith in his heart to believe which there is a God in heaven. We see he didn't get any confidence from anyone around him because no one could believe anything.

The people were living with him; they were all atheists. So, in fact, it should be God Himself will bring a revelation about Himself to him by His presence.

The Word said; faith comes by hearing the Word of God. As a matter of fact, when God spoke to him, it means God spoken the Word to him. The Word is God, and He is the Spirit. The other people were surrounding him without faith in God.

How wonderful is it that God has chosen Noah? It had given him great favor from God that he would have to love and to obey His command?

It should be a desire in everyone's life that we can walk with humility that He would choose us to be His favorite one. At the beginning of the Old Testament is revealing a compelling picture of Noah's faith and is one of the most compassionate hearts to obey God.

Preaching with Confidence:
Noah became excited and confident to preach a message of righteousness and judgment. He was on fire to carry a message of justice. God protected him along with seven others when he brought a flood on the earth upon ungodly people.

He was preaching about the coming judgment of God. The Lord had then a lot of patience with the situation all these years. It almost takes one hundred and twenty years of tolerance, as we read in Genesis 6.

Noah was building the ark for nearly 120 years. At the same time, Noah was building the ark and preaching all these years. But no one could be interested in hearing the message of God. I guess there was no enthusiasm because they were blind in spirit.

Having a doubt:

In the same situation, we have today when we speak the Word or preaching with the Fire of God. The people are not excited about hearing about God. I will guess that at the same feeling, Noah had doubted why these people are not coming back to God. No one can force the faith in God inside people's hearts. Noah did what is right in the sight of God; he did his part. God saw everything and every person who did not believe the God of Heaven.

The Lord knew that he could do something about corrupt people. The Word said God spoke to Noah; the time is near that human life comes to an end. The people were enjoying themselves by their own desire and having an experience of adultery, murderers, evil lifestyle, idol worshipers. The more corrupted mindset has occurred.

Preacher of Righteousness:

It characterizes Noah in the second Peter as he was "A Preacher of Righteousness." In that sense, he was a preacher? Even though the people were there watching him by day, by month, and years of hard labor. They came around him; maybe he was keeping everything in himself.

"and did not spare the ancient world, but saved Noah, one of eight people, a preacher of righteousness, bringing in the flood on the world of the ungodly." 2 Peter 2:5, NKJV.

But his commitment and his work on the Ark would tell a message of God. He would have been his testimony as a Preacher of Righteousness.

The theory of Noah comes to us, and he declared his zeal in the plan of God. He tried presenting both a warning of God's judgment and a message of salvation. Some believe that he had the truth from God in his message for corrupted people around him. I guess people asked themselves why Noah is building up a huge Ark?

The people began to laugh and to mock at him. Why does he build an Ark with no reason? Then Noah was preaching with the Fire of Holy Spirit to lost souls to repent. It would surely qualify with his authority of redemption, just like Jesus was teaching to lost sheep.

Final Word:

Noah's Flood shows us two facts about the character of God towards us. He was waiting patiently for the people would have to repent. They would come back to worship Him in the Spirit and Truth. The heart of every man was very cold and not ready to receive God's love and kindness.

We see the Word said, God was watching them from Heaven for a long time. How the people were living, but they have not opened their hearts, minds to God.

They have committed sins against God. He was furious with sin, and they should have to be punished soon. At the same time, we believe that He loves us, and He sends us a plan of salvation if we will simply repent and turn our hearts to Him.

• CHAPTER 2 •

The Ministry of Abraham

WE WILL LOOK AT the life and the ministry of Abraham. We want to continue going deep into the Word; however, we cannot find any place that Abraham preached or taught the Word of God. According to the book of Galatians said, God preached the Gospel to Abraham in advance.

"**And the Scripture, foreseeing that God would justify the Gentiles by faith, *preached the gospel to Abraham beforehand*, saying, in you, all the nations shall be blessed.**" Galatians 3:8, NKJV.

We will study the ministry of Abraham. I realize this statement involves an authoritative word of encouragement for us to become energetic followers of God. We would trust God in our everyday faith and walking with God, just like Abraham did. So, he goes on into a glorious journey of life, changing to a mighty ministry of faith.

Story of Abraham:
This is the story of Abraham's life, and his father, Terah, had three sons, Abram, Nehor, Haran. They lived in Ur of the Chaldeans. Terah took his son Abraham and his wife Sarah, grandson Lot, the son of Haran. They settled down in the city called Haran with all his family. Terah, the father of Abraham, died in Haran.

God revealed to him to leave his home, Haran. Abraham has received a call from God to leave His father's home. He had the heart to obey God's plan. He stepped out in faithful submission to the call of God, for he could hear and discern God's voice.

Abraham took his wife, Sarah, likewise, recognized as Sarai along with his nephew, Lot, and with all his wealth that they have received from God. He will bless all the people of the earth through Abraham. He moved in the land of

Canaan, which God has now given to Abraham and his descendant.

Abraham heard from God by faith that there was a promise coming over him. First, God placed Abraham in the Fire of His presence to understand how to obtain all the Promises.

The Lord God said:
- I will establish a great nation through Abraham.
- I will make his name great.
- I shall bless those who bless him; I shall curse those who curse him.
- I shall bless all the families of the earth through Abraham.
- I shall give all the Promise Land to Abraham; it will be given to him also to his offspring forever.
- I shall increase Abraham's descendant great as the sand of the earth and the stars.
- I shall make him a father of many nations.
- I shall bring out kings and kingdoms through Abraham.
- I shall establish an everlasting covenant with Abraham for his offspring.

- I shall be given the Land of Canaan to Abraham and his offspring, and it will be an everlasting possession.

As we notice, the name of Abraham was Abram means: "high father" thus, God has changed his name to a new name: Abraham, a father of many nations. When he turned ninety-nine years, he realized that he would never have a child from God with Sarah.

God established a covenant with him by processes of circumcision: the Jewish ceremony for a new baby boy representing the covenant between God and the Jews.

I wanted to share about Abraham's life and his journey to a new plan of God. I think he believed God; he preached to himself; he encouraged himself to move into a new future. The Word said: God preached the Gospel to Abraham, his heart stirred up, and his spirit was on fire for God.

That's why he obeyed God without knowing where his destination will be? He knew that by his faith, he would make it through to a new Land of prosperity with more blessings were waiting for him.

God Promised a Son:

God has promised Abraham to give him a promised son, and he had faith that Sarah would have a son. Soon later, three angels came to visit Abraham and Sarah. One of the angels informed Abraham that upon his return next year, Sarah would have a child.

While these three angels came, and they were standing at the tent entrance, Sarah heard the good news about her pregnancy in her old age. She laughed in herself about the matter of having a child at her age.

Sarah shortly became pregnant, and she delivered a son to Abraham, who was a covenant son from God, which had fulfilled at the perfect time. Abraham was a hundred years old, and he named his child, "Isaac."

As we learn, Abraham had two sons, the older son, Ishmael, means "God will hear." But the younger one, Isaac, means "laughter." God informed Abraham that his true covenant by establishing his divine heir upon Isaac. God's eternal covenant was through Isaac.

God promised to prepare his covenant and set up to make the everlasting covenant after

Abraham. Isaac would move up to the next stage of growth in life to be made into an important prospect in the divine plan of God. We recognize God's purpose was to provide the eternal covenant by Isaac.

God had to set up a covenant with Isaac and his true descendants after him. Through Isaac, an eternal covenant was established with the spiritual blessings arising from Abraham's trust and faith in God's promises about Isaac.

Jacob and Esau:
Let's view at the life of Isaac, how he had such a powerful influence over his family and two sons. I see Abraham has taught Isaac to have confidence and knowing God to observe God's law. The Bible said: Isaac was surely blessed with amazing possessions so that other nations around were extremely jealous of him. Isaac's wife, Rebekah, had twin sons, Jacob and Esau.

Isaac loved Esau, and he was becoming old, deciding to give him, birthright' blessings. Because Esau was older than Jacob, but Rebekah favored Jacob and helped him. She came up with an idea to trick Isaac to pass on the blessings from Esau to Jacob.

When Esau discovered that he had lost his blessings from his father, he decided to kill Jacob. Rebekah suggested sending Jacob away to her brother Laban far from other countries to stay over there until everything was getting peaceful.

We notice here about Jacob has been chosen by God. Jacob is the man to carry on with Abraham's covenant. He was entering the next God's chosen descendent by the sovereign plan of God. We recognize the hand of God upon Isaac is now passed onto Jacob to carry God's glory to Israel.

Despite Jacob's weakness, in fact, Jacob's name means "deceiver." He believed that God had called him to become a leader and carry out God's plan on earth. God doesn't look at any of our weaknesses or mistakes.

He looks at our courageous faith to declare God's name and to be a witness of His glory. After Isaac died at 180 years old, both of his sons Jacob and Esau grieved over their father.

Faith and Fire of God:

I think, if we are living according to the Word of God, we shall worship and praise His name without any shame. If we live by faith to not having doubt or fear, where God would take us? When God spoke to Abraham, maybe he had a fear and doubted about: is God speaking to me?

If God is really talking to me, I need a sign from God? It is natural to be afraid, and worry would come to us. But when He chooses us, and He makes way for us to know His plan, as long as we will follow His Word, we will never fail.

He knows, we go through the crisis in life; He loves us. He is responsible for our lives and to give us a victory. He will pour out the Fire of His presence over us. Then we will fire up to serve Him and love Him with all our hearts.

God wants us to give Him all we have in life, and he will do the rest. Being on Fire, we must preach to ourselves. I believe Abraham spoke loudly and walking with the Fire of God. The presence of God surrounded Abraham, God watching over Abraham's life. He was around him day by day.

How about us now, are we receiving all promises of God by faith? I would say, Yes. We are experiencing all promises of God that are manifesting every day. His Words are His promises.

We speak His Words and believing by faith. It shall come to us with all His blessings as Living Water, and it will overflow favor of God over us. Let's decree the good things that shall be established for us. In Jesus' name. Amen.

• CHAPTER 3 •

The Life of Joseph

THE COMPELLING STORY OF Joseph can establish an actual narrative in the Bible. There is no verse or no evidence that can be found in the book of Genesis that Joseph preached. But he had such a heart to serve; he knew that God had a plan for his life.

Joseph laid down his vision and his desire in the plan of God. He loved to be on Fire for achieving what God called him to be a leader. We experience that when God wants us to become a servant. He will prepare us; we will get ready, and we equip ourselves and obeying His Word.

It might be we go through the difficulty of life and having a tough time putting everything together. But everything can be possible with us, and He is able to make us strong to fulfill the vision.

I see Joseph received an excellent vision for the future; he was on fire; he couldn't keep to himself. He shared his dream with his brothers about his future leadership authority. He was walking and talking to himself in the presence of God. There is a lesson we will learn from the great story of Joseph.

We read Joseph's life, which God permitted an authority of leadership to be given to him. God trusted him to make history. We go further to describe more about this enthusiastic man, and how he handled all of his crisis, how he made it.

Joseph knew that he needs to grow up, not be afraid of any circumstance. He had to trust God; He allowed those situations that happened in his life. God would give him the authority to be used for the glory of God.

We recognized those times about Joseph had a bad feeling; he had doubted, and sometimes he wanted to quit. He built his faith by identifying God; he was still walking and living under the anointing of God. He accepted a call for carrying out the strategy of God's plan.

The Story of Joseph:
Let's look at Joseph's life; he became the chosen son because he was the first-born son of Rachel. Jacob loved him. His father made a unique gift in the design of a lavish coat for Joseph. This coat made with many colors, it was beautiful and fit on him.

By making him a special son and he received a coat which was still a symbol of superiority on that day, his father sincerely recognized him. His brothers were not glad about their father showed him a favor on Joseph.

His brothers became extremely jealous of him because Joseph had a dream. He shared his dream to his family that someday in the future, they are surrendering themselves under his authority. So, they will find a way to end his life, and his brothers were making fun of him. They planned in the field to kill him, but he trusted his family.

Sold Him as a Slave:

One day in the field, one of Joseph's brothers, Judah, proposed throwing him in the pit. They agreed to do so, and his older brother Reuben thought maybe to rescue him later. The other brothers saw the merchants from Egypt were passing by, and they were going back to Egypt.

These brothers shared with them about selling Joseph, they made a deal, and they sold Joseph as a slave to these merchants. They took Joseph as a slave into the land of Egypt.

Reuben came later to rescue his brother, but it was too late. They went to their father Jacob and told him what happened to Joseph. They said; the wild animals killed him in the field. They took Joseph's coat with the blood of an animal that they handed over to their father. Jacob deeply wept over his son Joseph and cry out for his life.

So, after a long trip, these Egyptian merchants arrived back home. They sold Joseph as a slave to a high-ranking Egyptian named Potiphar. He gave Joseph to rule over his household as a supervisor to oversee all his possessions. Potiphar entrusted him in all his house tasks.

Joseph in Prison:
He was exceedingly knowledgeable at his outstanding work. So, Potiphar's wife was seeking to seduce him, he rejected her, and he tried to slip away from her not to be trapped. But he took off, and she blamed him with false accusation to Potiphar, and he put him in jail. Joseph was an innocent man, but God has used him with many good things in prison for about 13 years.

They were two men in prison along with Joseph, and they shared their dream, he interpreted for them. One of them was the cupbearer of Pharaoh's palace. Joseph had interpreted his dream for him; then, after a while, he got freed from prison. Joseph told him, remember me when you go back to Pharaoh palace! Joseph has not lost his hope and his Fire for God.

Interpreted the Dream:
We learn here what powerful authority God granted to Joseph over a gift of the interpretation

of a dream. God allowed him to become ruler over the people. After two years, the Pharaoh had a dream. He couldn't find anyone to reveal the understanding of the vision. His cupbearer remembered Joseph in prison, who helped him to solve his problem.

He advised Pharaoh to call for him. He interpreted Pharaoh's dream; so, there will be seven year's plentiful harvest, and after seven years of famine will take place. He instructed them to store all grain and crops that they can survive over the next seven years of famine.

The Pharaoh couldn't find any wise man to handle and manage all properties. He determined to put Joseph in charge of all authorities. Joseph became the second in command in Egypt.

The Fire of God lived inside Joseph's gift to be able to understand the future. Let's ask the Lord Jesus releases His presence would come down to surrender us. We will hear His voice and listening to His words carefully.

Famine Began:

When the famine started and turned into drought in the land of Canaan. Jacob and his family had everything to live in the time of famine. He sent his sons to Egypt to bring some grain and food because there was no place can be found except in Egypt. All of Jacob's sons traveled in the desert without Benjamin on a long journey to Egypt.

They tried searching for food; so, they brought in a request to Joseph's attention that some men showed up from some foreigners. These men came from the land of Canaan to pick up some grain and food. Joseph recognized them as who they were.

Egyptian soldiers accused them of being spies, but Joseph had a thought; he planned an idea for his brothers, for they couldn't recognize him either.

Joseph ordered them to bring in the younger brother here, and he kept one of their brothers, Simon until they come back. Jacob allowed Benjamin to travel with them to Egypt to show them; they are not spies; they came only for grain and food.

Joseph Recognized his Brothers:
We realize here that Joseph had a passion for living with the fire of God, and he put his faith to work. He wanted to accomplish the task. Joseph found out that his brothers came back from their long journey, and they brought their brother.

Joseph ordered; Simon should be free to be united with his brothers. He organized a gathering with a good supper before he showed up to the place that they should meet together.

He noticed that his own brother Benjamin came along with them. He comes out of his chamber, and they bowed down to him, that is, prophecy has been fulfilled.

"And when Joseph came home, they brought him the present which was in their hand into the house, and bowed down before him to the earth." Genesis 43:26, NKJV.

Joseph still needed to know that his brothers have changed in their hearts, and they turned into godly men. He determined to make the right decision, and he arranged to put their money in their sacks. They put a silver cup in

Benjamin's sack, so they were on the road going out of Egypt.

Joseph sent some soldiers to go after them that they may bring them back to him again. They discovered that they had a silver cup in Benjamin's sack that they had stolen.

Joseph said I would keep him here that you may leave to your homeland. Judah begged him not to keep Benjamin because if he does, their father might die from grief.

Joseph Revealed to His Brothers:
Finally, after all the things they went through with crises. Joseph revealed himself to his brothers.

"Then Joseph could not restrain himself before all those who stood by him, and he cried out, "Make everyone go out from me!" So, no one stood with him while Joseph made himself known to his brothers. And he wept aloud, and the Egyptians and the house of Pharaoh heard it." Genesis 45:1–3, NKJV.

He wept with them and said to them, **"But as for you, you meant evil against me; but God meant it for good, in order to bring it about as it**

is this day, to save many people alive." Genesis 50:20, NKJV.

Joseph advised them to go back home and to bring his father with all his household back to Egypt. Jacob arrived with all his families to Egypt to meet Joseph. Jacob has settled down along with his twelve sons for the rest of his life until he died.

We understand here that "they did for evil, but God turn around for good." We desire to look up our eyes and concentrate on the God of Israel that He is surrounding us with His grace and blessing.

Here we know the Fire of God has been released into the authority of Joseph to complete an outstanding task. He was very sincere to go into the plan to lead and to finish it for the glory of God.

CHAPTER 4

The Mission of Moses

Let us study the mission of Moses, who had a fire of God, was burning in his life. The text shows us that Moses was a man of faith brought to action. He carried such a heavy burden to set his people free and to serve God. Moses was one of the strong men of faith who had confidence in the Old Testament.

We cannot find any place in the five books of Moses that he preached, but we found out he blessed the people of Israel before he passed away.

Moses' Final Blessing over Israel:
Moses had an impressive speech and gave a great blessing to the Tribes of Israel. We see

Moses committed to releasing God's blessings over his people; we read from the book of Deuteronomy, chapter 33.

In his statement, Moses advised the people they look up to the God of Israel. He will remind them of all the good works of God, what He has done in the past.

They may remember, God is good, and He is faithful. Also, warning them to follow and obeying all of God's commandments, God wanted to give good fortune to His people. Then he did a prophecy for each of the twelve tribes of Israel.

We want to look at the life of Moses. God's fire appeared in Moses's life, and the glory of God came around him so that even people could recognize God's power in his life.

He had a beautiful experience in the past at a young age; he paid no attention to his childhood luxury palace. He had all of his great pleasures for the sake of God's call upon his life, but he turned over to God. He understood there is a better life ahead of him.

Moses had a conviction for the rest of his life that God will be with him in time of his needs. He recognized Him; he needs God's protection and guidance with His presence to take them to victory.

God has already made a perfect relationship with him. He supplied all the people's provisions and with good health to live and to serve Him.

Once we move forward going into a pleasant experience with God. He has more plans and more surprises for us, it is just a matter of time. Moses had a fire to hear and to recognize the voice of God. He instructed his people from the Ten Commandments to live by the law of God.

We learn from Moses's authority, which God had prepared him to move on into the work of God under His presence. Moses had messages to communicate with his people. The God of Israel has established; the Law of Moses.

In evidence, it was allowed to reveal God's revelation to Israel. They sought God and accepted Him. They received redemption based upon doing their obedience to the law.

Fire in Burning Bush:
God had a plan to call Moses that he became His servant to deliver his people; they were crying out to God. He heard their petition; He wants

to prepare Moses to set His people free from Egypt. Moses was shepherding his father-in-law's sheep in the land of Midian.

When the Lord has called Moses to come up the mountain to meet with God, Moses did not expect to see the Fire. The Lord wanted to make a new relationship with him, and He needed to speak with Moses. He wanted to assure him that He heard the cry of His people. He promised Moses to set His people free from bondage.

The Lord instructed Moses not to be afraid of the future challenge of a long journey. Suddenly Moses saw the burning bush was near to him. But he saw the fire, but the bush was not burning.

Then he realized that the Lord had manifested His presence through Fire. So, he went down on his face. He could see the Fire and heard the voice of God, and the Lord spoke to him through the Fire.

"And the Angel of the Lord appeared to him in a flame of fire from the midst of a bush. So he looked, and behold, the bush was burning with fire, but the bush was not consumed." Exodus 3:2, NKJV.

The Pillar of Fire:
At the time, Exodus of the children of Israel leaving the land of Egypt. They needed the most guidance from God evermore. They didn't know where they were traveling in the desert by day or night. There was not any sign to lead them in the right direction to the Promise's Land.

The Lord has manifested His presence and His Glory as the God of Israel to His people. According to Exodus, the pillar of the cloud was watching over the Israelites. *The pillar of Fire* guides them through the night.

"And the Lord went before them by day in a pillar of cloud to lead the way, and by night in a pillar of fire to give them light, so as to go by day and night. He did not take away the pillar of cloud by day or the pillar of fire by night from before the people." Exodus 13:21-22, NKJV.

The Cloud and the Glory:
The cloud represents the Glory of God, and it's said: the cloud covered the tabernacle of meeting. Even when Moses could not enter the tabernacle of meeting, the Glory filled and rested upon the tabernacle. When the priests came

out, and the Glory of the Lord filled the house of God.

The Fire came down to make light by night, to make the people of Israel easy to their journey. So, the Glory was as the cloud by day, and the Fire was as the presence of God came down by night.

"For the cloud of the Lord was above the tabernacle by day, and fire was over it by night, in the sight of all the house of Israel, throughout all their journeys." Exodus 40:38, NKJV.

God's People Suffering:
Israel has settled down for going under the authority of God. Since it had been formed for the times of Moses. He could look back all the years how his families, his people were suffering under Pharaoh's reign in Egypt. He wanted to make a change to their destiny, and he needed to do something about it. I believe he opens his heart to seek God of his forefathers, which it has taught him.

He knew God could do anything; he was seeking God to rescue his people in Egypt. Searching God was an excellent way to experience His presence. God loves to perform a miracle, and He will involve himself in any situation. The Word said if we seek Him, and we will find Him.

The Lord spoke to Moses later, and he declared God's Word to the people that they must worship God, follow Him, and obey Him. God had equipped them with more talents and skills for Jewish people. The provisions of God had created wealth to set up the tent of meeting and agreeing to God's plan. As we review, people had no wish to surrender their lives to the Lord and Moses.

People Complained:
An entire generation had murmured, opposed to God. But many perished before a new population could go in the Promised Land. God protected them in the wilderness and showed them how to worship and obey God for forty years.

Moses taught the people about the God of Abraham. He guided them that the Lord God had a great message for them. He would deliver them from the suffering of slavery after 400 years in Egypt. God had to work on with signs and wonders and kept His words through

Moses. God only completed the plan through Moses' leadership.

There has never, therefore, raised a humble leader in Israel like Moses. In whom, the Lord allowed him, and God met Moses face to face. It will be desirable to see more leaders can show God's Fire as Moses has presented, which we could learn from him.

We must honor the authority of God's chosen leader. For not going against any leader, we might be going against God Himself.

Fire from the Lord:
When the people began to complain about their hardships, the Word said: The Lord was very displeased. He sent out His fire from heaven to consume them in the whole camp. The fire of God was among them, and the people cried out and asking Moses that he would ask God to bring the fire down.

"Now when the people complained, it displeased the Lord; for the Lord heard it, and His anger was aroused. So, the fire of the Lord burned among them, and consumed some in

the outskirts of the camp." Numbers 11:1-3, NKJV.

Moses Humbled:

Although Moses was very trustworthy in the sight of God, he acknowledges his influence with compassion and encouragement.

The Word said: Moses was very humble, **"Now the man Moses was very humble, more than all men who were on the face of the earth."** Numbers 12:3, NKJV.

We see he continues with Aaron and Miriam from starting to fulfillment through the event. Likewise, when they move forward to make more exciting adventures together. The story moves on as Moses showed his leadership and authority with Miriam.

Moses carried the commitment to seek God for his sister to heal her, even though Miriam made a mistake to come against her brother Moses. He pleads with God to heal Miriam's body, and the Lord hears his prayer to heal and bringing her back after seven days, the punishment of being sent away from the tent.

"So, Miriam was shut out of the camp seven days, and the people did not journey till Miriam was brought in again." Numbers 12:13-15, NKJV.

In every situation, Moses went through; he has such faith and humility before God. He believes that he can carry out the fire of God will come down from heaven over the people of God. We really need to have strength and grace to walk in the spirit of humility.

We will realize we are fulfilling this character when we identify ourselves, that we can encourage someone. Then we lift them up in prayer, and the Lord visit them where they are.

Moses saw the Promised Land:

We understand, God has honored Moses as the head and leader of the Israelites. The someone else whom God has appointed and delivered His people out of Egyptian bondage. God had another plan for him; the Lord did not allow him to enter the Promised Land. We studied the Word said: God has shown the Promised Land to Moses from a far distance; He said: as I promised to your forefathers.

And He did not allow Moses to enter the Land. I believe he was standing by and dreaming to see the land that he was awaiting and fought for the land in many years. But God and Moses were standing on the mountains; He said: I will show you; I allow you to see it, but you will not enter the land.

I have chosen another person who is Joshua to carry the task to take my people into Promise Land.

"Then the Lord said to him, "This is the land of which I swore to give Abraham, Isaac, and Jacob, saying, 'I will give it to your descendants.' I have caused you to see it with your eyes, but you shall not cross over there." Deuteronomy 34:4, NKJV.

Then, while Moses was up on Mountain Moab with God, he died. The Word said: God buried him up there in Moab. He was 120 years old.

"And He buried him in a valley in the land of Moab, opposite Beth Peor; but no one knows his grave to this day." Deuteronomy 34:6, NKJV.

• CHAPTER 5 •

The Courage of Joshua

WE WILL LOOK AT the courage of Joshua, and he was ready to use his Godly ambition. He wanted to make a difference in the future generations of Israel. As we describe, Joshua has been very dedicated to God from a young age. I understand that the rule of Moses' authority influenced him and converted him into a good commander.

God has chosen Joshua to lead the Israelites into the Promise Land. It is a remarkable strength to train people in the right direction, according to God's plan. When God calls us, He will prepare the way; then, He will be our guider.

Joshua carried out the people of Israelites with reaching the goal and conquering the land of promise which God has prepared for them. It reveals his personality and how he was walking and living under the presence of God.

His life and ministry have touched many lives. When Moses has assigned Joshua and Caleb, they became the spies for inspecting the land. Therefore, they brought back great news of the Promised land.

Double Portion of Fire:
We must remind ourselves that when the Fire of God came down on Joshua, he received a double portion of anointing all over him. The authority of God came to teach him to become a servant with power.

He was carrying a great determination to declare the truth, challenging the people to move forward. Joshua learned what God instructed him to assemble people to follow, to worship with their hearts.

Afterward, he was an associate with Moses, who changed into the ruler of Israel after Moses passed away. As God called him because of his faithfulness of heart remaining steadfast with Moses. God has passed on Moses's authority over Joshua. He grew into a leader of the Israelite people, conquered Canaan, and divided the land between the tribes of Israel.

Two Spies and Rahab:
Joshua has appointed two spies to be sent out into the Promised Land. They both went and met Rahab. Unfortunately, the Word of God has not revealed the name of two spies that Joshua assigned them to Jericho. They both came back with a great report to Joshua.

Indeed, they would say: **"And they said to Joshua, "Truly the Lord has delivered all the land into our hands, for indeed all the inhabitants of the country are fainthearted because of us,"** Joshua 2:24, NKJV.

After the strike and conquered the city, they had victory over Jericho. When Joshua has allowed these two spies, they met Rehab from the town of Jericho. Now, after victory, they delivered all her families out of the city alive as they promised. When Israel captured the city to spare their lives in Jericho.

Jericho Wall Collapsed:
Let's look at Joshua's courage and depending on God. He walked by faith and getting training through Moses, and he was a greatly obedient insight of God. Moses has entrusted him to give the assignment to do the job. When the time arrived, Joshua has received an order from God to march around Jericho for seven days. By faith, the Wall fell down.

The Word said: **"And the seventh time it happened, when the priests blew the trumpets, that Joshua said to the people: "Shout, for the Lord has given you the city."** Joshua 6:16, NKJV.

It's a miracle of God that the wall of Jericho crushed by the power of God. He directed Joshua to do wonders along with all Israelites. We learn here crushing and breaking the massive wall is a picture of a big mountain of our crisis today.

It could be a terrible dilemma and a hard situation in our lives, but nothing is impossible with God. He can do anything for us, Amen.

Crossing the Jordan:
Anytime God is making something good by His presence to create a change. What we require to

do just seek His direction. The only thing is we will do to submit ourselves under His plans and moving forward by faith. It may life become impossible for us, but God is always possible.

Look at crossing the Jordan River: Then Joshua spoke to the priests, saying, **"Take up the ark of the covenant and cross over before the people." So, they took up the ark of the covenant and went before the people."** Joshua 3:6, NKJV.

"Now, therefore, take for yourselves twelve men from the tribes of Israel, one man from every tribe." Joshua 3:12 NKJV.

There was a stream river that reached not to be possible to cross.

The people couldn't find out how to cross the Jordan, but they recognized it on the other side appeared to be "Promised Land" a new home was waiting for them. But the Jordan River was a flowing stream with the people's future with a great destiny.

The Land was particularly forthcoming with spiritual prosperity and miracles. The people were purifying themselves to honor God, to observe the priests who were carrying the Ark of the covenant.

Looking at the Ark should cross through the river by God's presence. The nations glanced at the leadership of the Lord has created for them. When the priests lifted the Ark stepped into the water, at that moment, the water stopped running in the river.

"Then the priests who bore the ark of the covenant of the Lord stood firm on dry ground in the midst of the Jordan; and all Israel crossed over on dry ground until all the people had crossed completely over the Jordan." Joshua 3:17, NKJV.

It's the action of God's work to do wonders in the front of His people that He is faithful to His Word.

Achan's Sin:

The battle of Ai brought defeat to Israelites; it was a matter of warning to the Israelites. Joshua was wondering what caused the downfall.

Joshua pursued the Lord, **"Then Joshua tore his clothes, and fell to the earth on his face before the ark of the Lord until evening, he and** the elders of Israel; and they put dust on their heads." Joshua 7:6, NKJV.

The Lord informed Joshua that there is a sin has committed in the camp. The Lord wants to remove the sin and destroy it. The disgraceful of Achan brought sin to Israelites was the awareness to people.

God was furious because, **"Israel has sinned, and they have also transgressed My covenant which I commanded them. For they have even taken some of the accursed things and have both stolen and deceived; and they have also put it among their own stuff."** Joshua 7:11, NKJV.

Achan replied, **"And Achan answered Joshua and said, "Indeed I have sinned against the Lord God of Israel, and this is what I have done."** Joshua 7:20, NKJV.

Achan's way of life and his sins cleaned away from the camp with a fair act by all Israelites. Then God granted them victory over their enemy as God directed Joshua to force the people in battle and kills the people of Ai.

The city was wiped out and burned to the ground. They killed the king of Ai and all their men on the battlefield.

The Sun Remains Still:
It's incredible about the manifestations of God's presence appears to allow the sun to stand still:
"So, the sun stood still,
And the moon stopped,
Till the people had revenge,
Upon their enemies." Joshua 10:13, NKJV.

God was watching, and He was in the middle of the plan. God was overseeing his people who were fighting to defeat their enemies. Surely, the Lord was looking after Joshua and His people! God has miraculously given over twenty-four hours of daylight to Israelites to end the fight.

The only way God has empowered them to remain stable. Because God wanted to demonstrate His Glory over his warriors. The Israelites attacked against the five kings in the battleground, and they wiped out their enemies. We read a compelling story from Joshua 10:1-18.

To refer mark to confirm the condition as an eclipse that allowed the display of a long day. Directly, some evidence of an eclipse producing the bright light in the space. It could have performed the day should take place longer than usual in which the sunlight did not set. God created the scene to move forward precisely with Joshua's prayer and a time of his desire to be achieved to victory.

Seven Years Battle:
Within seven years of battle, the people continued to win every war with their enemies. Over throughout years, the Israelites had trials, struggles, and fighting against enemies. God has made a way to conquer.

The Lord has granted great leadership to Joshua, and he brought the Israelites into the right direction. They had seized 31 kings and their land. It was now the Israelites occupied the Promised Land.

"the king of Tirzah, one—all the kings, thirty-one." Joshua 12:24, NKJV.

The Lord directed Joshua by His great authority to divide the land into twelve tribes of Israel. God gave all abilities; the courage, the knowledge, the provision. God has made a great warfighter, going to war against their enemies with Joshua. He experienced all Israelites desired to fulfill their purposes.

The presence of God can bring miracle the same for us today, as He made for His people. He will bring every favor of what we need to accomplish the tasks.

Joshua devoted his way of life to remain faithful in battles to secure territory for the Israelites. It wasn't a peaceful task for him to serve so many men. He had such obstacles to carried out his call with the help of the Lord. God knew that Joshua was becoming old. Joshua completed the plan of God, and he became blessed with prosperity.

Joshua accomplished his work. God reassured Moses that all the Israelites would have to settle down in the Promised Land. Joshua advises the people to remember God what He has done for them. God gave Joshua a long life, and he passed away at the age of 110 years.

Serving with the Fire of God:
When God called Joshua to serve, He rewarded him with the strength to carry out the plan of God. We learn from the Word, **"Now, therefore, fear the Lord, serve Him in sincerity and in truth, and put away the gods which your**

fathers served on the other side of the River and in Egypt. Serve the Lord!" Joshua 24:14, NKJV.

When we honor Him with our attitude and believing Him by faith, what He can do miracles in our midst.

- "Having faith and believing," that He is able, and He is sustaining us to serve Him with an excellent spirit.
- "Having sincerity to serve Him," we offer our life, what we have received from Him. It may be our life be used for His Glory. He can perform many miracles through us.
- "Serve Him alone only," we desire to have the heart to worship One true God. Not having other "gods" beside the God of Israel. He is the Holy, perfect, and He is a loving God.

• CHAPTER 6 •

The Twelve Judges

WE WILL LOOK AT these great warriors who gave their lives to God. They were called and chosen to serve and defend the people. God raised up twelve judges to deliver the people from the hand of their enemies and to save the people of Israel.

After the death of Joshua, the people would not want to follow God's law; they've chosen to worship other gods. They changed their hearts into idol-worshipers. People rebelled against God and did not wish to continue to have true faith in God.

So, the tribes quarreled among themselves and forced to battle for some parts of the land. But they couldn't prevail in the fight without God. The enemy attacked them, and God brought oppression against Israel to show them to trust Him.

Any time the people rejected to pursue the God of Israel, their enemies defeated them, and then they would come to repent. The nation called upon the name of God many times, and God permitted them to get victory on the battlefield.

The bad news was that the people would always return to worship other gods again. The Fire of God is the mighty presence of the sovereign Lord is always restoring His people. Looking at these fighters and the heroes of faith were ready to exalt the name of God.

As we know, the Fire represents; the presence of God raised up twelve judges to deliver the people from their enemies and to take care of the nation of Israel.

Othniel:

The first judge was Othniel, son of Kenaz. He was Caleb's younger brother. God raised him up as a commander and a judge in Israel. He seized the king of Mesopotamia, and the Israelites encountered God and peace.

He accomplished the task in the land. Othniel's influence reached out for a long time, as he proceeded to go to war for the nations, and they had peace for forty years.

"When the children of Israel cried out to the Lord, the Lord raised up a deliverer for the children of Israel, who delivered them: Othniel the son of Kenaz, Caleb's younger brother. The Spirit of the Lord came upon him, and he judged Israel. He went out to war, and the Lord delivered Cushan-Rishathaim king of Mesopotamia into his hand; and his hand prevailed over Cushan-Rishathaim. So the land had rest for forty years. Then Othniel the son of Kenaz died." Judges 3:9–11, NKJV.

Ehud:
The second judge was Ehud, and he was left-handed. After Othniel died, the nations transferred their faith and followed Eglon, the king of Moab. After they had served him for eighteen years, they cried out to God to set them free. The

Lord chooses Ehud. He made a sword and slew King Eglon.

Ehud fled, and he went to blow up a trumpet in the mountains. The Israelites attacked them and massacred many men of Moab. They had peace for the next eighty years. He declared freedom to the nation of Israel.

"follow me, for the Lord has given your enemies to you." Judges 3:12–30, NKJV.

Shamgar:

The third judge was Shamgar, about whom we have no details of his life. There is only one short verse included in the Scriptures about his victory. The verse mentions that Shamgar was the son of Anath. He struck six hundred men and killed all the Philistines with an ox goad 'usually recognized as a good stick.' He later delivered the people from their enemies.

He defended God's people from any attack. We cannot find any chapter, how many years God assigned Shamgar to be judge over His people.

"After him was Shamgar the son of Anath, who killed six hundred men of the Philistines

with an ox goad; and he also delivered Israel."
Judges 3:31, NKJV.

Deborah:

The fourth judge was Deborah; she was the only female judge, a prophetess of Israel. We will study the life of Deborah, and she was married to Lapidoth. The people couldn't succeed in the fight because the enemy was stronger than them. She had an extraordinary fire of God with a passion for serving.

She had a zeal to fight the enemy as a leader for the nation in the time of suffering. But Deborah was a commander to the army of Israelites, and she could hear the voice of the Lord when God ordered her to attack Sisera.

Deborah directed the people to defeat Sisera because God was taking care of the site and leading them. He wanted to teach the people how to build up their faith into fearless warriors. He reminds them they should be more reliable than their enemies.

No matter how many armies they had or how mighty their swords are! When God revealed to Deborah to move forward by the Spirit of God to kill the giants. They prevailed, and they won a great victory on the battlefield.

We understand here that Deborah had carried the fire of God to kill the vast armies of the enemy. Others came along with her were afraid to attack. The people could not move forward until Deborah gave a command to attack Sisera. Deborah trusted God and carried out an excellent call to win the enemy.

Maybe we are also afraid in some situations in our lives, but we must move forward to attack the devil. We must remember that the devil is a liar and a deceiver who seeks to kill and destroy every one of us.

Gideon:

The fifth judge was Gideon. Let's view the story of Gideon, as stated in the Bible. Gideon was a great military man and a commander of the army. He wanted to bring God's mission to deliver and accomplish a remarkable job for his people.

For seven years, the people had struggled with many invasions from the Midianites, Amalekites, and other Eastern foreigners in the land. The enemy had destroyed all their crops and cattle. People had suffered and forgotten their faith in God.

They started to worship other gods, **"So Israel was greatly impoverished because of the Midianites, and the children of Israel cried out to the Lord."** Judges 6:6, NKJV.

But now they cried out to the God of Israel for leadership. God appointed a prophet to advise the people who had forsaken Him in the past. The people should be reminded that there is a God in heaven.

"Also I said to you, "I am the Lord your God; do not fear the gods of the Amorites, in whose land you dwell." But you have not obeyed My voice." Judges 6:8–10, NKJV.

God prepared Gideon, the fifth judge of Israel. He was very obedient and submissive to the God of Israel. He had a fantastic encounter with God, and the fear of God was all over him. The Bible states that Gideon demolished the idols and all other gods.

The people turned out to honor and worship the One true God again. Because of his faithfulness and fear of God. Gideon received more blessings, and the people request him to be a commander and a leader over Israel.

The inspiring words will show us a profound message about Gideon was devoted to God. He was not a quitter. Gideon was loyal to God's call. Gideon had a fear of God toward what God instructed him to do. Gideon realized that God was magnificent and perfect in every situation of life.

Tola:

The sixth judge was Tola, the son of Puah. God has established His leadership after the death of Abimelech. We could find no information about the life of Tola; he is the least documented as a judge. There are no reported actions of Tola.

But we do know that he carried out what God called him to do. He was to serve in wisdom and reconciliation for the nations of Israel. He ruled for twenty-three years.

"After Abimelech there arose to save Israel Tola the son of Puah, the son of Dodo, a man of Issachar; and he dwelt in Shamir in the mountains of Ephraim. He judged Israel twenty-three

years; and he died and was buried in Shamir."
Judges 10:1–2, NKJV.

Jair:
The seventh judge was Jair, and there are only a few verses that would talk about this judge. The Word says that Jair had thirty sons, and they traveled with a large family to thirty cities. They were riding with thirty donkeys!

It reveals to us that God granted thirty years of peace for Israel, during the time of Jair was the judge over the nations. He was a judge and a leader for twenty-two years.

"After him arose Jair, a Gileadite; and he judged Israel twenty-two years. Now he had thirty sons who rode on thirty donkeys; they also had thirty towns, which are called "Havoth Jair" to this day, which are in the land of Gilead. And Jair died and was buried in Camon." Judges 10:3–5, NKJV.

Jephthah:
The eighth judge was Jephthah, who came from Gilead. He was born from another woman. They forced him to leave when his brothers threw him

out of the house. Because they believed he was an improper child. He will not get any inheritance from his family. The Bible specifies that he moved to the region of Tob, and he settled there. He became a mighty fighter.

While he was there, he gathered a gang of scoundrels around him, and they followed him. He fought in the battle, and they prevailed. Jephthah was only a judge for six years.

"Then Jephthah fled from his brothers and dwelt in the land of Tob; and worthless men banded together with Jephthah and went out raiding with him." Judges 11:1–3, NKJV.

Ibzan:

The ninth judge was Ibzan, he served Israel, and God blessed him with many sons and daughters. He offered his thirty sons and thirty daughters in marriage from outside of his tribe. Ibzan brought in thirty women for his thirty sons!

As we learn, Ibzan was born, and his life ended in the same city. His sixty sons and daughters blessed him with tremendous changes in his life. He has created many alliances with other Israelites.

It would have increased his effectiveness as a leader. He was a judge for seven years. Then Ibzan passed away and was buried in Bethlehem.

"After him, Ibzan of Bethlehem judged Israel. He had thirty sons. And he gave away thirty daughters in marriage, and brought in thirty daughters from elsewhere for his sons. He judged Israel seven years. Then Ibzan died and was buried at Bethlehem. "Judges 12:8–10, NKJV.

Elon:

The tenth judge was Elon. There is no report about his leadership, and he used his authority to lead Israel. Elon served Israel for ten years, and he was from the tribe of Zebulun. When Elon passed away, he was buried in Aijalon in the land of Zebulun.

"After him, Elon the Zebulunite judged Israel. He judged Israel ten years. And Elon the Zebulunite died and was buried at Aijalon in the country of Zebulun." Judges 12:11–12, NKJV.

Abdon:
The eleventh judge was Abdon. He was a son of Hillel from Pirathon, who served Israel. God blessed his household with forty sons and thirty grandsons. He was very wealthy and had a great family; they rode on seventy donkeys.

Abdon was from the tribe of Ephraim. He would have been a prosperous man who was known in his day. When Abdon passed away, he was buried at Pirathon in Ephraim in the hill country of the Amalekites. He ruled Israel for eight years.

"After him, Abdon the son of Hillel the Pirathonite judged Israel. He had forty sons and thirty grandsons, who rode on seventy young donkeys. He judged Israel eight years. Then Abdon the son of Hillel the Pirathonite died and was buried in Pirathon in the land of Ephraim, in the mountains of the Amalekites." Judges 12:13–15, NKJV.

Samson:
The twelfth judge was Samson. His life story turns out with the message of his birth. As we know, an angel of the Lord who appeared to his

father, Manoah, and his wife. She will have a son who then gave birth to Samson.

He was the toughest man in the Bible. Unfortunately, he was making the wrong choice in his life and ministry. He ends up in his own death. He had victory over his enemies, the Philistines.

God will carry out His plans even through sinful men. Samson willingly moved into places where he opened his heart to sin. But nevertheless, God entrusted him for his accomplishment.

Samson was a man of strong bodily power. The Spirit of God moved upon him on many occasions. The Lord gave him tremendous courage to attack the Philistines. These people were the enemy of the Israelites. Although Samson was falling in love with the woman Delilah who was from Philistines.

Samson's story would result in fleshly temptation. It produces destruction and disobedience. God uses sinful people to carry out His will with His mercy. Samson served as a judge in Israel for twenty years.

Inspiring Message:
- The encouraging message here is why the people were seeking their own opinions of how to worship other gods to satisfy their lives. It shows us that seeking God requires faith and confidence in His Word.
- God has called each of these men and one woman to serve under the Fire of God. They were all ready to obey and to fight for their people to transform the nation and bringing the people back to God.
- People were committing sins against the law of God. But God remembered the covenant He had made with His people and with Abraham that He would take care of His people.
- It brings our obedience to His leadership and guidance. God does not want us to be idol-worshipers or to follow after other gods. If we study His commandments, we will rise up into successful and prosperous people.

• CHAPTER 7 •

God Sent Fire from Heaven

When God is sending down His glory as a flaming fire, the Fire of God is the Fire of His presence, His power, and His Glory. The Fire of purity that anoints us and will strengthen us. The Fire that consumes and devours the evil actions.

What the Word of God said about a consuming fire: He can overcome the enemies that are stronger than us. God has the power to demolish and to cast out every demonic activity to those who hold against us. God can make the triumph over any enemy.

"For the Lord, your God is a consuming fire, a jealous God." Deuteronomy 4:24, NKJV.

Fire is operated in the bible to represent God's presence. We learn in the book of Exodus that God showed up to Moses as Fire.

"And the Angel of the Lord appeared to him in a flame of fire from the midst of a bush. So he looked, and behold, the bush was burning with fire, but the bush was not consumed. Then Moses said, I will now turn aside and see this great sight, why the bush does not burn." Exodus 3:2-6, NKJV.

Fire is intended to burn, cleanse, destroy, demolish, and consumes all impurity. We learn the scriptures that on the day of Pentecost, ***the fire of God*** manifested by His Spirit in the upper room. We studied how God calls Himself as a consuming fire.

We again understand that God sent ***fire from heaven*** to burn the sacrifice on the Altar. Making pure and burning the sacrifice so that it would make perfect unto God.

We read in this verse says: When all the people of Israel watched by their own eyes, ***the fire of God*** coming down and the magnificent presence of the Lord filling the Temple. Then the people saw it, they fell down on their faces to the ground and worshiped the God of Israel and praised the Lord.

"When all the children of Israel saw how the fire came down, and the glory of the Lord on the temple, they bowed their faces to the ground on the pavement and worshiped and praised the Lord, saying:

"For He is good, For His mercy endures forever." 2 Chronicles 7:3, NKJV.

The Pillar of Fire:
At the time, Exodus of the children of Israel leaving the land of Egypt. They needed the most guidance from God evermore. They didn't know where they were traveling in the desert by day or night. There was not any sign to lead them in the right direction to the Promise's Land.

The Lord has manifested His presence and His Glory as the God of Israel to His people. According to Exodus, *the pillar of Fire* was watching over the Israelites and guide them. The pillar of cloud settled and stayed at the door of the tabernacle, and the Lord spoke to Moses.

All the people looked at the pillar of the cloud remain at the tabernacle door. The people in their tent praised and worshiped the God of Israel.

"And the Lord went before them by day in a pillar of cloud to lead the way, and by night in a pillar of fire to give them light, so as to go by day and night. He did not take away the pillar of cloud by day or the pillar of fire by night from before the people." Exodus 13:21-22, NKJV.

Fire with Smoke on the Mountain:
On the third day in the morning, the people heard thundering and lightning. There was a thick cloud on the mountain. Suddenly the people heard the sound of the trumpet was very loud that the people who trembled in the camp. Moses brought the people out of their camp to meet with God.

They could stand at the foot of the mountain. It surrendered the whole Mount Sinai with smoke. Because the presence of the Lord moves upon *the fire*, the people could see the smoke and furnace top of the mountain quaked.

According to the Word of God, the trumpet blasted and sounded long and louder. God answered Moses with the sound of a trumpet.

I would say: God Himself blasted the trumpet, and the sound was the voice of God.

"Now Mount Sinai was completely in smoke, because the Lord descended upon it in fire. Its smoke ascended like the smoke of a furnace, and the entire mountain quaked greatly. And when the blast of the trumpet sounded long and became louder and louder, Moses spoke, and God answered him by voice." Exodus 19:18-19, NKJV.

The Fire on the Mountain:
When the time of a new visitation of Moses came with God, and the Lord called him up on the mountain to meet him. The moment Moses went up there, the Glory of the Lord came, and the cloud covered the top mountain. Moses stayed for six days, and on the seven's day, God called Moses out, in the midst of the cloud.

The Glory of the Lord has revealed His Fire on the top of the mountain. The people have seen the Fire and the Glory in their eyes. The Glory of the Lord just like consuming *Fire of God* on top of the mountain. Where all the children of Israel were standing and looking up, they saw the Fire of God.

"The sight of the glory of the Lord was like a consuming fire on the top of the mountain in the eyes of the children of Israel." Exodus 24:17, NKJV.

Fire from the Lord:
When the people began to complain about their hardships, the Word said: The Lord was very displeased. He sent out His fire from heaven to consume them in the whole camp. The fire of God was among them, and the people cried out and asking Moses that he would ask God to bring the fire down.

"Now when the people complained, it displeased the Lord; for the Lord heard it, and His anger was aroused. So, the fire of the Lord burned among them, and consumed some in the outskirts of the camp." Numbers 11:1-3, NKJV.

250 Men Consumed by Fire:
These three men, Korah, Dathan, and Abiram, revolted against Moses, and they gathered

250 men with them. The Lord heard and saw them. The Lord displeased with these men were against His servant Moses. *The fire of the Lord* came out to consume these 250 men who were offering the incense.

"And a fire came out from the Lord and consumed the two hundred and fifty men who were offering incense." Numbers 16:35, NKJV.

The Fire Consumed Nadab and Abihu:
The sons of Aaron were Nadab and Abihu to bring their offering. They took their censer and set fire to it; they put incense on it. Then they offered profane fire before the Lord.

The Word said; it was not the command of the Lord. So, *the fire of God* sent out from His presence to consume them. The Lord struck them with His presence; they died just right there.

"Then Nadab and Abihu, the sons of Aaron, each took his censer and put fire in it, put incense on it, and offered profane fire before the Lord, which He had not commanded them. So, fire went out from the Lord and devoured

them, and they died before the Lord." Leviticus 10:1-2, NKJV.

Aaron Offering Consumed:
It was the time of offering to the Lord. Moses commanded Aaron to give his offering on the Alter, make atonement for himself and his people. They killed a bull and a ram as sacrifices for the peace offering.

They killed a goat for the sin offering. They brought grain a handful of it for the grain offering burned on the altar. After all offerings: the sin offering, the burnt offering, and peace offerings have presented on the Alter.

"Moses and Aaron went into the tabernacle of meeting," Leviticus 9:23, NKJV.

They stepped out to bless the people. Suddenly, *the fire of the Lord* came out and consumed the burnt offering. People saw what happened, they shouted, they went to the knees on their faces.

"and fire came out from before the Lord and consumed the burnt offering and the fat on the altar. When all the people saw it, they shouted and fell on their faces." Leviticus 9:22-24, NKJV.

People Afraid of God's Presence:
The people were afraid of God's voice because they knew His voice is His presence. The people gathered from every tribe and elders; they saw the mountain was burning with the fire. They knew this is the presence of God.

They saw His Glory, His greatness; they heard His powerful voice in the midst of ***the Fire.***

"And you said: 'Surely the Lord our God has shown us His glory and His greatness, and we have heard His voice from the midst of the fire. We have seen this day that God speaks with man; yet he still lives." Deuteronomy 5:24, NKJV.

The Angel Ascended in the Flame:
When the angel of the Lord gave Manoah good news about his wife will deliver a chosen child whose name is Samson. They invited the angel to have a meal with them.

Angel of the Lord said: No, I cannot have any meal, but you may offer your burnt offering unto the Lord. So, Manoah picked up a young goat with the grain offering.

Manoah presented an offering upon the rock to the Lord. Meanwhile, Manoah and his wife were looking at Alter. The angel of the Lord was in ***the flame of the Alter*** and ascended into heaven. Manoah and his wife fell down on their faces to the ground.

"it happened as the flame went up toward heaven from the altar—the Angel of the Lord ascended in the flame of the altar! When Manoah and his wife saw this, they fell on their faces to the ground." Judges 13:19-20, NKJV.

Sacrifice Offering:

Elijah, the prophet, came to bring sacrifice offering unto the Lord. He said; You are the God of Abraham, Isaac, Jacob. You may reveal yourself in this day to your people that there is a mighty God in Israel. Elijah said; you will show yourself to these people around me that I am your servant. You bring these people's hearts back to yourself.

The Word said; ***the Fire of God*** fell down from heaven and consumed the burnt sacrifice. The Fire burned the wood, the stones, and dust.

"Then the fire of the Lord fell and burned up the sacrifice, the wood, the stones and the soil, and also licked up the water in the trench." 1 Kings 18:36-38, NKJV.

From the Midst of the Fire:

We see God began to speak to His people, and the Lord wanted to talk with them face to face from the midst of the Fire.

"The Lord talked with you face to face on the mountain from the midst of the fire." Deuteronomy 5:4, NKJV.

The Lord has chosen Moses to stand between the people and God. Because the people were afraid to stand in front of the Fire of God.

"I stood between the Lord and you at that time, to declare to you the word of the Lord; for you were afraid because of the fire, and you did not go up the mountain." Deuteronomy 5:5, NKJV.

Consuming Fire:

It might be you have heard about the word: God is a *consuming fire*. It means that he can overcome or conquer every enemy or overpower any attack that is trying to come against us, or it may greater than us. God has the authority to strike them out those who stand against us.

God can make a victory over any opposition. When we are living under the pressure of devil's lies to sickness, and with wrong thoughts. God will handle those spirits of depression and sins.

The Bible frequently attributes to God as a *"consuming fire."* The Glory of God as a ***consuming fire*** consists of the concept of God's protection. He is the divine character; His judgment is justice upon those who resist Him.

"For the Lord your God is a consuming fire, a jealous God." Deuteronomy 4:24, NKJV.

It means precisely that a fire entirely consumes, or it will burn and destroys their enemies. We read this verse:

"Therefore understand today that the Lord your God is He who goes over before you as a consuming fire. He will destroy them and bring them down before you; so you shall drive them out and destroy them quickly, as the Lord has said to you." Deuteronomy 9:3, NKJV.

Fire from the Lord:
When the people began to complain about their hardships, the Word said: the Lord was very displeased. He sent out ***His fire*** from heaven to consume them in the whole camp. ***The fire of God*** was among them, and the people cried out and asking Moses that he would ask God to bring ***the fire*** down.

"Now when the people complained, it displeased the Lord, for the Lord heard it, and His anger was aroused. So, the fire of the Lord burned among them and consumed some in the outskirts of the camp." Numbers 11:1-3, NKJV.

God's Holiness:
God's purity is the reason for His existence, the nature and the essence of His Glory is a consuming fire. It will burn up everything unholy. The holiness of God is the part of His character that most divides Him from sinful man.

Isaiah would say, we all will tremble before Him: "Who can experience with the consuming fire? Who can survive with everlasting burning?" It is saying; that only the righteous person can resist the consuming fire of God's wrath.

Because sin is destruction to God's holiness, but Isaiah still encourages us. There is no measure of our own goodness, and human righteousness can be sufficient. We read in this verse;

"The sinners in Zion are afraid;
Fearfulness has seized the hypocrites:
Who among us shall dwell with the devouring fire? Who among us shall dwell with everlasting burnings?" Isaiah 64:6, NKJV.

First Fire:

We see in the story of Job that he lost everything. As *the fire came down from heaven,* burned up all Job's flocks. There was a warning strike from Satan, but he was doing with the approval of God.

"While he was still speaking, another also came and said, "The fire of God fell from heaven and burned up the sheep and the servants, and consumed them; and I alone have escaped to tell you!" Job 1:16. NKJV.

It was a hardship given by God, and, as a result, Job brought glory to God. On the other part of his tests, the Lord enriched Job with even more flocks than before.

"Now the Lord blessed the latter days of Job more than his beginning; for he had fourteen thousand sheep, six thousand camels, one thousand yoke of oxen, and one thousand female donkeys." Job 42:12. NKJV.

Burning the City:
God has condemned Sodom and Gomorrah of people's horrible sins. The main reason God sent fiery sulfur on the cities because people had a desire to live with the spirit of homosexuality of being attracted to other people. The city got wiped out with all of its inhabitants.

The fire has sent from heaven as rained brimstone over the city of Sodom and Gomorrah. There was a massive *fire burning* down that destroyed the entire city.

"Then the Lord rained brimstone and fire on Sodom and Gomorrah, from the Lord out of the heavens." Genesis 19:24, NKJV.

Captains and his Men Consumed by the Fire:
Ahaziah fell on the lattice of his upper room got injured in Samaria. Ahaziah said, there is no God in Israel. Therefore, he sent a messenger to Baal-Zebub, the god of Ekron, to help him for getting recover from his injury. The Lord heard it and made a judgment upon Ahaziah.

He sent a Captain of fifty men to meet Elijah; they told Elijah: he needs to come down to meet the king. Elijah said to Captain: if I am a man of God, let ***the fire of the Lord*** will consume you and your men. According to the word of Elijah: The fire of God came down and destroyed them all.

Ahaziah sent another captain with fifty men again to Elijah, and then they were consumed by ***the fire of the Lord*** again. Ahaziah sends the third Captain with fifty men to Elijah, and the Captain fell on his knees; he pleaded for mercy from him and his men not to be consumed by the fire of the Lord.

Then the angel of the Lord appeared and spoke to Elijah to go with them to meet Ahaziah. He went to see him; Elijah spoke the word of the Lord to Ahaziah, that he didn't believe that there is a God in Israel; therefore, you indeed die.

Then he said to him because you have sent messengers to seek of Baal-Zebub, the god of Ekron. Because, you thought, there is no God in Israel to believe in His word?

"Look, fire has come down from heaven and burned up the first two captains of fifties with their fifties. But let my life now be precious in your sight." 2 Kings 1:14, NKJV.

Fire on the Alter for David:
Because David recorded a census of the people, God was displeased with him, and He wanted to strike Israel. But the Lord gave three choices to David, so, these choices were: famine, invasion, and plague were given to choose.

David recognized his mistake, and he accepted the plague, and the Lord struck seventy thousand people perished in Israel. Then, the angel of the Lord directed Gad to say to David that he should go to make an altar to the Lord on the threshing floor of Ornan the Jebusite.

David spoke to Ornan, would you give me the place of this threshing floor, that I may make an altar onto the Lord. You shall give it to me at the full price, that the Lord God will remove the trouble may be cleared away from the people.

So, David gave Ornan six hundred shekels of gold by value for the place. And David established an altar to the Lord, and he presented burnt offerings and peace offerings. He called unto the Lord, and the Lord God acknowledged him from heaven by *fire on the altar* of burnt offering.

"And David built there an altar to the Lord, and offered burnt offerings and peace offerings, and called on the Lord; and He answered him from heaven by fire on the altar of burnt offering." 1 Chronicles 21:26, NKJV.

The Glory Entered the House:
After King Solomon dedicated the House of God with prayer, and he sacrificed sheep and oxen. The end of his prayer, *the fire of God* came down from heaven consumed the burnt offering and the sacrifices. All the people began to offer their sacrifices before the Lord. Even the priests couldn't enter the House.

The Glory of the Lord came down, filled the House, and the Spirit of the Lord poured out in the House of God. All the people were standing around the house, and they saw *the fire of God*. They bowed down on their faces, worshipping and praising the God of Israel.

"When all the children of Israel saw how the fire came down, and the glory of the Lord on the temple, they bowed their faces to the ground on the pavement, and worshiped and praised the Lord, saying: "For He is good, for His mercy endures forever." 2 Chronicles 7:1-3, NKJV.

Fire on Mount Carmel:

Ahab sent all prophets and the prophet Elijah to bring a sacrifice on the Alter on Mount Carmel. There were almost four hundred and fifty men of Baal's prophets. But Elijah was alone by himself as a prophet of Israel. Baal's prophets started to prepare their Alter with one bull cutting in pieces, woods, but no fire underwood.

They called the god of Baal to send fire to burn the woods to make a sacrifice offering for them. No answer! They ask again until noontime and evening, but no response from the god of Baal.

Elijah stood up to prepare the Alter with twelve stones represent the twelve tribes of the sons of Jacob. He put the wood, cutting bull in pieces, pouring four waterpots with water on the Alter.

In the evening at the time of the offering, Elijah prayed that the Lord brings these people's hearts back to Himself. Then *the fire of the Lord* fell and burnt sacrifice on the Alter.

"Then the fire of the Lord fell and consumed the burnt sacrifice, and the wood and the stones and the dust, and it licked up the water that was in the trench." 1 Kings 18:20-38, NKJV.

Judgment on Assyria:

When Isaiah said about the destruction of the Assyrians in the book of Isaiah, chapter 30:27-30. Isaiah prophesied the true Word of the living God who can come against God's people.

Isaiah points out two facts:

1. The tongue of the Lord is as a consuming fire:

"Behold, the name of the Lord comes from afar,

Burning with His anger,

And His burden is heavy;
His lips are full of indignation,
And *His tongue like a devouring fire."* Isaiah 30:27, NKJV.

2. His arm is moving down with wrathful anger:

"The Lord will cause His glorious voice to be heard,
And show *the descent of His arm*,
With the indignation of His anger
And the flame of a devouring fire,
With scattering, tempest, and hailstones." Isaiah 30:30, NKJV.

The Fire on the Alter:

God commanded Moses to instruct Aaron and his sons to perform the law of burnt offering. The Lord called for them to make a burnt offering on the hearth of Alter all night until morning. The Lord wanted to reveal His presence as the Fire is burning on the Alter.

That the Fire will remind the people which they need his Glory, and they will see God's presence in the fire. They would have to worship and to glorify God.

The priest brought wood and lay down on the Alter every morning. But the Fire of God was there on the Alter and keeping the fire on all the time.

"And *the fire on the altar* shall be kept burning on it; it shall not be put out. And the priest shall burn wood on it every morning, and lay the burnt offering in order on it; and he shall burn on it the fat of the peace offerings. *A fire shall always be burning on the altar*; it shall never go out." Leviticus 6:12-13, NKJV.

Elijah Ascends to Heaven:
The time of Elijah came that the Lord should take him up to heaven. Elijah and Elisha were together and wanted to cross Jordan. They stood there, Elijah took his mantle and rolled it up, then struck the water got divided. So, they passed it to dry ground.

Elijah asked Elisha, what can I serve you before I go away from you? Elisha replied; let me have a double portion of your spirit! Suddenly, it happened, *a chariot of fire* arrived with **horses of fire** by a whirlwind, Elijah went up into heaven.

"Then it happened, as they continued on and talked, that suddenly a chariot of fire appeared with horses of fire and separated the two of them; and Elijah went up by a whirlwind into heaven." 2 Kings 2:10-11, NKJV.

Faith and Fire in the Furnace:

As we read about these three Jewish brave men: Shadrach, Meshach, and Abednego did not bow themselves to worship other gods, which King Nebuchadnezzar made a law. When everyone hears the sound of music, they must bow down and worship the golden image.

These three men were working over the tasks of the province of Babylon. They forwarded a message to the King that these men will not worship the golden image. He called these men; he asked them why you will not worship the golden image?

They said: we serve our God only. He will send them into a fiery fire furnace, and they said: our God will deliver us from the fire. They placed them in the furnace; then, the King looked inside; he said: I see four persons are there, and I see the One who is the Son of God.

The King brought back from the fiery furnace with no burning in their body. He will praise God of Israel.

"And the satraps, administrators, governors, and the king's counselors gathered together, and they saw these men on whose bodies the fire had no power; the hair of their head was not singed nor were their garments affected, and the smell of fire was not on them." Daniel 3:26-27, NKJV.

- CHAPTER 8 -

The Holy Spirit like a Fire

FIRE IS A MARVELOUS image of the work of the Holy Spirit. The Spirit of Fire is operating in many ways. He draws God's presence to us, He brings God's passion, and He reveals God's purity. The Word is the Spirit; the Word of God is full of power and Glory. The Holy Spirit is the presence of God as He resides in the believer's heart.

As I mentioned before, in the Old Testament, God displayed His presence to His people the Israelites by surrounding the tabernacle with fire.

According to the book of Numbers 9:15, it would say: **"Now on the day that the tabernacle was raised up, the cloud covered the tabernacle,**

the tent of the Testimony; from evening until morning it was above the tabernacle like the appearance of fire." Numbers 9:15, NKJV.

Now, let's look at the New Testament, which will give us an insight into the Fire of the Holy Spirit. We found in the book of Hebrews 12:29, **"For our God is a consuming fire."**

Fire is a form of the heavenly presence with the power of God. Fire is a purifier, for judgments and protection.

Baptized with the Holy Spirit and Fire:
John the Baptist came to preach the repentance of sins. He gathered the crowd to baptize them with water in the Jordan River. He proclaimed that there is another One who is mighty than I to baptize you with the Holy Spirit and *Fire*.

This scripture is the evidence of His outpouring of *the Fire*, and His presence over His Church. We read:

"I indeed baptize you with water unto repentance, but He who is coming after me is mightier than I, whose sandals I am not worthy to carry. He will baptize you with the Holy Spirit and fire." Matthew 3:11, NKJV.

Fire on the Pentecost:
Let's find out, what is the meaning of the word Pentecost? The Word Pentecostal is from the Greek word "fiftieth," or "Shavuot." Probably it is very familiar to all of us to celebrate Easter, Jesus has risen from the dead. As we know, we celebrate Jesus's death and resurrection.

In fact, after Easter, they waited to experience Pentecost. Suddenly, as on the fiftieth day, the outpouring of the Fire of the Holy Spirit occurred. Mainly the birth of the church found on the day of Pentecost fulfilled by wind and fire.

Jesus said to His disciples concerning the Holy Spirit. When the Holy Spirit appeared to them, as He had encouraged his followers to wait for their counselor.

Fire Descended:
When the time of the Fire of Holy Spirit descended upon the disciples and followers about 120 in Jerusalem. Jews and the people coming from every nation were all gathered together in one accord in the Upper Room. They were worshipping the Lord Jesus in one spirit, and

they were in one heart to adore the Lord God of Israel.

Suddenly, the Fire of the Holy Spirit entered into the gathering as a rushing wind. No one could control the crowd, but the presence of the Holy Spirit was there to control the meeting. The Fire descended from heaven, and all the people spoke other languages.

The Holy Spirit enabled them and filled them up with new tongues of fire falling on all the disciples. They began to speak in the native languages of the people.

Everyone could hear the language, also could understand their own language, and they were astonished. The people thought the disciples of Jesus drank in wine.

"And there were dwelling in Jerusalem Jews, devout men, from every nation under heaven. And when this sound occurred, the multitude came together, and were confused, because everyone heard them speak in his own language." Acts 2:5-6, NKJV.

Baptized with the Holy Spirit:

Those followers of Jesus were expecting to receive the baptism of the Holy Spirit on the Day of Pentecostal. It was a promise from the Lord Jesus for an outpouring of the Holy Spirit in the first chapter of the book of Acts. The Lord has fulfilled His promise to the church.

The Word said: When the Holy Spirit comes on you, and He empowers you to preach the Word of God with boldness. It means; there should be a baptism of the Holy Spirit for all believers to obtain more power and authority to share the Gospel to lost souls.

That's why the Lord knew His disciples and followers needed more courage. He came to strengthen them from the Fire.

"But you shall receive power when the Holy Spirit has come upon you; and you shall be witnesses to Me in Jerusalem, and in all Judea and Samaria, and to the end of the earth." Acts 1:8, NKJV.

Peter Preached:

After the Holy Spirit filled the house with His Fire on the Day of Pentecost. Peter was the only

Apostles who stood up to preach the Word of God to the Gentile. He preached with the boldness of the Fire of God. Many heard the Good News of the Lord, and about 3,000 new souls were saved.

"But Peter, standing up with the eleven, raised his voice and said to them, "Men of Judea and all who dwell in Jerusalem, let this be known to you, and heed my words." Acts 2:14, NKJV.

As we know, Peter received a fresh anointing of the Holy Spirit. He was the first disciple of Jesus, and he also became the first preacher of the Day of Pentecostal. There were people all around gathered for a Jewish Feast. It is called the Feast of Shavuot or Pentecost.

We read in the book Leviticus 23:15, said: **"And you shall count for yourselves from the day after the Sabbath, from the day that you brought the sheaf of the wave offering: seven Sabbaths shall be completed."**

This is the Feast of Weeks or First Harvest. This feast was taking place seven weeks or 50 days. It connected the feast after the Feast First

Fruits, which becomes the day after the weekly Sabbath.

Fire is God's Presence:
Throughout human history, God appeared in the form of fire and glory. The definition of glory is that form of perfection, which typically contributes to admiration, honor, and praise.

We could see the patterns of the burning bush and the pillar of fire, moving the people in the wilderness. The Holy Spirit is as fire and glory, and the disciples heard as the mighty rushing wind.

There was the fire of God's presence for His people to rest upon the twelve apostles. It's revealing that the Holy Spirit will fill up each believer and empowering them to perform the work of God.

Prayed with Boldness and Fire:
Peter and John were standing to preach the resurrection of Jesus, and they preached the Word with the power of God. There is no other name that has been given to us except the name of Jesus we shall be saved. The elders and priests of

the temple were anxious, and they tried to stop Peter and John.

They took them to jail until the next day when the elders and the ruler of the law came to the temple; they brought Peter and John. They asked: In what power and what name do you do this? Then Peter said, by the name of Jesus Christ of Nazareth, that you crucified Him, and God raised Him from death.

"let it be known to you all, and to all the people of Israel, that by the name of Jesus Christ of Nazareth, whom you crucified, whom God raised from the dead, by Him this man stands here before you whole." Acts 4:10, NKJV.

So, these elders found nothing to accuse them, and they ordered to let them go free. But others came saying; if these men go back to the people in Jerusalem, which they have made signs and wonders before, they will do again. The elders threatened them, said to Peter and John, you may go, but you will promise not to use the name of Jesus again.

They said: we cannot help it because of what we have seen and what we heard of the name of Jesus! Peter and John went back to their members in the congregation. They prayed with boldness. They prayed, Lord, send your mighty Spirit to heal the sick and save lost souls.

After this prayer: they went out to preach the eternal Word of God with signs and wonders. They preached with a great boldness never before. O' Lord, may Your anointing of the Holy Spirit shall come down on us to preach the salvation of the Lord.

"After they prayed, the place where they were meeting was shaken. And they were all filled with the Holy Spirit and spoke the word of God boldly." Acts 4:31, NKJV.

Some Baptized with the Fire:
As we read the Word and we experience, all believers can have a baptism with the Holy Spirit. We must remember, the Baptism of the Holy Spirit is available for everyone. But not every believer is willing to get baptized with Fire.

As I mentioned before, the Holy Spirit is a Fire that showers heavily upon us and when the fire comes inside us. We receive a great passion, a great desire, and a great love for serving.

Nothing can hold us back to do the Will of God. The burning of the fire is there to anoint us for the ministry. The authority of God will help us to carry out the great commission to preach and teach the Word of God. God has chosen His servants to be hungry and to go everywhere what the Lord leads them.

Some are ready to lay down their lives in the will of God. Only a few special servants of God appointed by Jesus. Some will give all in life by faith to the Lord for His plan. He chooses His people to establish the Kingdom of God on earth.

I tell you the truth; we will follow His Spirit to accomplish the work of His Kingdom. It will remind us of the plan of the Holy Spirit leads us into glorious power in the Lord. By the passion which we have, and He gives us the pure Fire, draws us in full authority.

A Christian believer cannot control himself in preaching because of the anointing of God is upon him. The Holy Spirit motivates us to teach and preach the Word. He empowers us to give up our entire life for the ministry.

The Lord Jesus chooses the person who appointed even before his birth, but He watches over His servant to grow up to get prepared. At his appointed time to baptize him with fire to receive the full anointing of His divine task.

When the time is right, He pours out the Holy Spirit to instruct the man and woman of God into a worldwide ministry. These servants will be ready to preach with signs and wonders to perform healing, miracles, deliverance in the name of Jesus.

Holy Spirit's Fire is beyond all Powers:
When the fire grows in a person's spirit, the personality will change immediately. Everything in the world turns into a worthless meaning; even his or her own life will entirely focus on the Lord Jesus. The person would have to carry the glorious call of God to reach out to the Great Commission.

I have seen many servants of God were willing to die for the sake of the gospel. When the moment we get baptized with fire, the only desire we must do is to minister to lost souls. May we find ourselves in the places that the Holy Spirit will lead us in the streets or everywhere.

The Lord loves our obedient; then He shows us his direction. Our obedience will honor and glorify the Lord. He will lead us to where to preach the gospel.

Churches Not Opening to the Fire:
Many congregations today do not allow themselves into a great awaking of the Spirit. They don't wish to engage themselves with these God's chosen servants.

These godly servants can bring a new revival to support the church for spreading the Gospel. But some leaders of the churches will use their spiritual authority to the wrong path.

Today we see in many churches have closed their doors of opportunities to prospective servants. Some churches must recognize God's servants who have a great anointing of the Fire of God upon their personal life and leadership.

Apostle Peter Received Fire:
We study in the book of Acts after Peter received the Fire of God. He receives doubled portions of

the anointing of God to preach after the Holy Spirit baptized him along with others. He declared the Word of Salvation that even Peter was a man who could not stay in crowded people and, but he stood up to preach to multitudes.

He was frightened, and he had no courage in himself. He cared for his life that he could not give up his life for the ministry. We remember he denied Jesus in front of the Lord three times. But those things happened to him before he was baptized with the Holy Spirit on the Day of Pentecost.

After Peter had an alive encounter with the Lord Jesus by walking and hearing the teaching of Jesus. He wanted to get a new visitation of the Fire of God. He received the empowerment and boldness in the Pentecost.

The Word said Peter was the first Apostle stood up to preach the Gospel. Peter had no fear or no shame to declare the eternal Word of God. The multitudes were hearing the Word of God.

He knew his life has changed for better, and to live in Christ shall be glorious. He also ready to go to a new challenge of life to confront any opposition in Jews community.

He Baptized me with the Fire:

When I got born-again about 35 years ago by His Grace and mercy, my Pentecostal church taught me how to get baptized in the Holy Spirit. I didn't know what's it all about! But I was hungry as a new believer to receive all His blessings. When the time came, and on that day, some godly ministries laid hands on me.

I didn't know where I was in the spirit; I began to cry in my heart. I became overwhelmed by His presence. I could sense He was filling me up with the Holy Spirit. He appeared to me.

Nothing is important in the world than His presence and His Glory. Everything in life is less necessary for me, not living with materials things today.

I know His Fire is burning in my bones and my spirit. His Kingdom is more meaningful than anything else in my life. I am carrying my call to serve God's people and preaching His powerful Word to lost souls. It is an honor to fulfill my assignment.

His Fire of Spirit heals many sicknesses and a broken heart. His Fire is burning inside me so profoundly. He called me into ministry and to heal all kinds of sickness.

I love to preach His Gospel to everywhere to any churches. He is leading me by His Spirit to other States and other nations or countries. Anywhere the Holy Spirit will lead me and open doors to proclaims His goodness.

Pray with Fire Burns Everything:
The fire of God is burning all of the sickness and problems in those faithful believers. Examine your prayer life if you feel that your prayer does not get through in the fire. If it is not allowing you to move up to the next level of spiritual maturity, and perhaps it needs more anointing of the Holy Spirit.

If you feel when you pray that your heart is empty, make sure that you are seeking your best, and you are pushing to the fire of the Spirit. I encourage you to ask the Holy Spirit to fire you up. Try praying and reading the Word at the same time.

If you are not baptized in the Holy Spirit, you probably need to be. Because when the Holy Spirit comes upon you. You will receive power and the fire of the Holy Spirit to empower you to witness. You can then pray in a new language of the Spirit for yourself and minister to someone by the boldness and authority of God.

God's plan in the Fire:
How can we identify God's plan in prayer? Many ask this question. The only way we can recognize God's plan is through His Word and the guidance of the Holy Spirit. Let's study the Word with enthusiasm in our situations and decree the plan in our daily lives.

Revealing His plan must only be through the leadership of the Holy Spirit because His Word is truth. The Holy Spirit will confirm to us through His Word or someone or a situation in our daily activities.

The Lord is using all kinds of circumstances around us to get our attention to Him. When we understand God's plan, and we know it right away. We will have peace about it. He is protecting us, and He will indeed bless us.

You would ask the Lord in prayer: Lord, reveal your plan in my life, and what do you want me to do in your Kingdom. Bring light in my pathway that you would take me into a great future. To find out how the spirit of God is speaking.

We must be grateful to His plan through His Word. It's also useful to see that someone is praying; it can deliver a prophetic Word to us. We would understand the fire of God to confirm what the Lord has prepared for us.

Fire makes a Dynamic Warrior:
To become a dynamic prayer warrior is required to get into the spirit of passion and having a desire to be used by Him. Make yourself available and tell Him, "Lord, here I am; use me." He is taking us to an unknown place to be a witness. He delivers people from the bondage of darkness into the light and heals a broken heart.

The fire of God brings glorious miracles for His honor. Step up to a new level of power so that you can rebuke the devil and remove him from any crisis or sickness from a Christian home. Today, many faithful Christian believers are very dedicated to come to church to serve any place in the Body of Christ.

But on the other hand, they're suffering in their problems, especially in sickness. All they do is to continue going to the doctor and the hospital to get recovered. It is God's will to get healed. We shall step up in faith, stand up in the gap for others, and intercede for the saints of God.

Fire with Anointing:
After I have been living for many years in the Lord, I understood the anointing of the Lord. I mentioned before, and I can tell you anointing means empowerment of the spirit of the Lord. The Holy Spirit is full of power to give us more authority to overcome every sickness, poverty, doubt, lack, weakness, anxiety, oppression, stress, confusion, depression.

"how God anointed Jesus of Nazareth with the Holy Spirit and with power, who went about doing good and healing all who were oppressed by the devil, for God was with Him." Acts 10:38, NKJV.

Also, the empowerment of the Holy Spirit will be released over us with more Fire of His presence to witness. The anointing will enable us to enforce every sickness to healing and to destroy sins.

In Acts 1:8, it says, **"But you shall receive power when the Holy Spirit has come upon you; and you shall be witnesses to Me in Jerusalem, and in all Judea and Samaria, and to the end of the earth."** NKJV.

His Flame of Fire:
We read in the book of Isaiah, and the Lord will come with *His Fire*, with His chariots just like a whirlwind. He does His anger with rage, and to rebuke with blazes of fire.

"For behold, the Lord will come with fire And with His chariots, like a whirlwind, To render His anger with fury, And His rebuke with flames of fire." Isaiah 66:15, NKJV.

There was lightning, thunderings from the throne, and it came with glorious sounds. It referred to seven lamps of fire, burning before the throne. There were the seven Spirits of God.

"And from the throne proceeded lightnings, thunderings, and voices. Seven lamps of fire were burning before the throne, which are the seven Spirits of God.", Revelation 4:5, NKJV.

The fire used for Eternal Punishment:
The Word of God clearly would say about the Fire will be used for eternal punishment. This scripture gives us a crucial detail of sinful human nature that will not allow a person to accept eternal life. Basically saying, those who reject to repent of their sinful lifestyles will have to experience eternal death in the lake of fire.

"But the cowardly, unbelieving, abominable, murderers, sexually immoral, sorcerers, idolaters, and all liars shall have their part in the lake which burns with fire and brimstone, which is the second death." Revelation 21:8, NKJV.

Throw Them into the Fire:
In this verse would say, is anyone who does not accept Jesus as Lord and Savior. The details of this verse should be followed. The burning of the dried branches of the real vine represents the ultimate judgment.

They will throw them into the Fire. When we accept Jesus as Lord in our hearts, and He taught us to abide in Him only.

"If anyone does not abide in Me, he is cast out as a branch and is withered; and they gather them and throw them into the fire, and they are burned." John 15:6, NKJV.

• CHAPTER 9 •

Baptism in the Holy Spirit

THE BAPTISM IN THE Holy Spirit prepares the followers of Jesus to empower them for a witness to lost souls and to have an experience with the Fire. The doctrine of the Baptism in the Holy Spirit to receive more power and to become a spirit-filled believer.

The promise of the Father has fulfilled to send the free gift of His power to all Christian believers. We read in the book of Acts said: John baptized you with the water, but you may wait for many days to get baptized with the Holy Spirit.

"for John truly baptized with water, but you shall be baptized with the Holy Spirit not many days from now." Acts 1:5, NKJV.

The purpose of baptism has made for us to live more with His power. It must be a real and true confession of faith in the Lord Jesus; they have had an experience as a born-again Christian. They have received Jesus as the Son of God and accepted Him as Lord and Savior. So, the Holy Spirit will come and dwell in our lives.

Baptized His followers:
One of the main goals was to baptize His disciples and followers to receive these characters: His power, boldness, courage, authority, strength, fearlessness, tenacity, steadfastness.

Those verses in the New Testament will testify that the Lord wanted to release His outpouring of His Spirit.

We read that the Lord Jesus has instructed them not to witness to anyone until they get baptized in the Holy Spirit. We see Jesus has started His teaching and His preaching until He had been "Anointed" with the Power and the Holy Spirit.

"The Spirit of the Lord is upon Me,
Because He has anointed Me

**To preach the gospel to the poor;
He has sent Me to heal the brokenhearted,
To proclaim liberty to the captives
And recovery of sight to the blind,
To set at liberty those who are oppressed."**
Luke 4:18, NKJV.

Clothed with Power:
Jesus said: I will send the promise of My Father, but you may stay in Jerusalem until you must be equipped with the power from on high. Jesus's disciples were alone without the Lord, and they had an enjoyable experience while Jesus was walking with them.

They had a lot of fear; they wanted to go out to preach with the Fire of God. But they needed to obey what the Lord told them to wait to be "Clothed with Power."

Because they've waited for the time of the outpouring of the Spirit of God. Jesus appears to His disciples after the resurrection. He said: peace unto you, My Father has sent me, and I will send you also to the entire world. He breathed on them, said: *"Receive the Holy Spirit."*

"So Jesus said to them again, "Peace to you! As the Father has sent Me, I also send you." And when He had said this, He breathed on them, and said to them, 'Receive the Holy Spirit'." John 20:21-22, NKJV.

Filled with the Holy Spirit:

The time of the Day of Pentecostal had come. They all had waited to have a new experience of His power with one accord in one place. Suddenly, a sound came down from heaven, as of a great rushing wind.

There was a Spirit of God filled the whole house where they gathered as the fire rested upon them. The Holy Spirit came to fill them up. They started to speak with other tongues, as the Spirit gave them.

"And suddenly there came a sound from heaven, as of a rushing mighty wind, and it filled the whole house where they were sitting." Acts 2:2, NKJV.

Speaking in other Tongues:

The manifestation of baptism in the Holy Spirit would have to speak in other tongues. Let's look at the Day of Pentecostal when a sound of new rushing wind came down on the gathering. The Spirit of God filled them up with the Holy Spirit. How can they know that they are baptized in the Holy Spirit?

The sign is the Spirit of God gave a new language to speak an unknown language. And to be a sign to them that they are baptized and filled with the power of God.

"And they were all filled with the Holy Spirit and began to speak with other tongues, as the Spirit gave them utterance." Acts 2:4, NKJV.

Boldness to Preach:
The boldness we will receive from Him would have an impact on our lives, and in our prayer life as well. To become a prayer warrior, we need to speak in tongue and seeking Him with our hearts.

He makes us bold to preach His Words. He will manifest His Glory through our lives to become pure and Holy in His presence.

We are becoming bold for giving prophetic words and releasing a prophecy word to someone or the church or a nation. The reason is, we get baptized in the Holy Spirit to receive boldness for preaching, teaching, witnessing, intercession prayer, hearing the voice of God.

"But you shall receive power when the Holy Spirit has come upon you; and you shall be witnesses to Me in Jerusalem, and in all Judea and Samaria, and to the end of the earth." Acts 1:8, NKJV.

More Result of Baptism:
Speaking in tongues can be very effective in the Prophetic spoken word to serve others. Today we are ministering among God's people. It would give these prophetic words to confirm in the person's life, which has already spoken before.

When we are speaking in other tongues all the time. Suddenly, the spirit will draw us to others to give the right word to encourage, edify, and comfort them.

"For he who speaks in a tongue does not speak to men but to God, for no one understands him; however, in the spirit he speaks mysteries. But he who prophesies speaks edification and

exhortation and comfort to men." 1 Corinthians 14:2-3, NKJV.

Speaking in tongues will strengthen our spirit to start declaring His name all the time. We learn how to make a declaration of praise. Our mouth shall be full of praise and to be filled with the word of grace to others.

"For they heard them speak with tongues and magnify God." Acts 10:46, NKJV.

When we speak in tongues, the Spirit of God revealing to us about if we are living in sin that we grieve the Holy Spirit. Sometimes we don't pay attention to the life we live every day.

It might we live in an immoral act; we try to hide those sins. The Holy Spirit is aware of it, and He is the One would have to show us how we can clean ourselves from sins.

There will be a proper check-up in our hearts going after His holiness. He is revealing a deeper awareness of God's judgment against our ungodliness lifestyle.

The deeper sins we are in, the more severe damage we can do in our own lives. Then we reap a terrible harvest. He is trying to reveal to us where is a lack. Because of His love toward us, He wants us to repent our sins, not to be condemned.

"And when He has come, He will convict the world of sin, and of righteousness, and of judgment." John 16:8, NKJV.

There will be a hunger for prayer that grows into our hearts by speaking in tongues to know God's Word and to experience Him better.

The Spirit of God will reveal to us what gifts and talents we have! He wants us to be used by Him. Speaking in tongues will bring revelation about our potential gifts and ministry in the Body of Christ.

"There are diversities of gifts, but the same Spirit. There are differences of ministries, but the same Lord. And there are diversities of activities, but it is the same God who works all in all. But the manifestation of the Spirit is given to each one for the profit of all." 1 Corinthians 12:4-7, NKJV.

Laid Hands to Receive:
When Philip preached the message of the Gospel, they were amazed to hear the Good News of the Kingdom of God. Those men and

women were baptized, then Simon also believed, he got baptized as well. He went out with Philip to see signs and miracles that what the Lord is doing among the people.

While the Apostles were in Jerusalem, they heard about how the Word of God has impacted the Samaria. They marveled with great joy; the people have responded to the message of the Gospel. They sent Peter and John to them that they may go to pray for the people, which God will do miracles through them again.

They went to Samaria; they expected that God would bring an outpouring of the Holy Spirit over the people. And the people got baptized in water, but they knew nothing about the baptism of the Holy Spirit. Then these Apostles laid hands on them; they receive the Holy Spirit.

So, the Lord can use lay hands on someone to baptize in the name of the Lord. In other times, the Lord will appear to an individual believer alone who is seeking the Lord. He will baptize him without laid hands on him. The Lord will visit us when we search for Him; He will meet us where we are!

"For as yet He had fallen upon none of them. They had only been baptized in the name of the Lord Jesus. Then they laid hands on them, and they received the Holy Spirit." Acts 8:16-17, NKJV.

Hunger to be Filled:

The Lord loves to fill us with His Word, with His presence, and with His peace. He is looking for those who are hungry to fill up their spirits with Fire. He loves to see that we are walking in His Grace and living with the Fire of the Spirit. We must have a desire to live and serve the people of God with His anointing.

We must have a deeper hunger for Him to read His Word and to pray in the spirit. The Word mentioned: Out of every person's heart will flow rivers of living water. Every person's heart would have hunger going after God. Humble heart shall be filled.

"He who believes in Me, as the Scripture has said, out of his heart will flow rivers of living water." John 7:38, NKJV.

At the same time, we get hungry in the spirit—we feel we are empty inside. So, we seek

Him and reading His Word to strengthen our spirit to become stronger. Hunger for God is not exciting for many Christian believers in this generation.

Unfortunately, people are hungry for unnecessary material ambitions to bring them into darkness. They will have temporary and short-time pleasures. But those things draw them to confusion and a lost world without eternal life in Christ.

We are hungry for other things, and the things of the world are drawing us to sin, and we're getting lost in this world. We need to turn our ambition around into a sincere desire to follow Him and run into **the fire** of the Holy Spirit.

Are we hungry or thirsty? I love this verse says that we must be thirsty and hungry for God. I wish everyone could have a great passion for being hungry for His presence and thirst for His Word. Because His Word is as a medicine in our body and to our soul and our spirit. His presence creates healing, and He perfects us for His glory.

"For He satisfies the longing soul, And fills the hungry soul with goodness." Psalm 107:9, NKJV.

This verse from the book of Matthew says that it blesses you to be hungry to know Him and seek Him for your life. Our faith grows and builds up in our heart by hearing Him and listening to His voice again. We would always be ready to pray in season and out of season.

"Blessed are those who hunger and thirst for righteousness, For they shall be filled." Matthew 5:6, NKJV.

I love the last phrase is! "Shall be filled." They shall be filled with the Holy Spirit and blessings and more miracles to come to us. Are we ready to receive grace and the abundant kindness of the Lord? He is pouring out from heaven to shower over us. Be ready to accept Him. in Jesus's name. Amen.

Fire with Prayer Answer:

I mean, sometime the Fire of God will bring an answer to our prayer. It comes down on us while we are praying a quick prayer or a long prayer. The Spirit knows when we are ready to change and getting ready to transfer into the realm of His Glory.

If we have a great passion for serving and longing to hear His voice to minister with prophetic words. We must pray in the spirit to praise and to worship Him with all our hearts. The answer is always ready for us when we come into His Glory and experience His Fire.

"If you then, being evil, know how to give good gifts to your children, how much more will your heavenly Father give the Holy Spirit to those who ask Him!" Luke 11:13, NKJV.

· CHAPTER 10 ·

Speaking in Tongues

THE PURPOSE BEHIND 'SPEAKING in tongues' is mentioned, which is to be one of God's gifts to Christian believers as the original manifestation of the baptism of the Holy Spirit.

Every believer can speak in supernatural languages given in the Day of Pentecostal by the Holy Spirit. We study there was an outpouring of the Spirit in the early days of the Church. They waited to be touched by the heavenly strength for every believer. There will not be any reason to be different now.

Speaking in tongues is a pure gift from the Lord. Some times people do not have the meaning of speaking in tongues. But on other occasions, we see some people are hungry for more power of God. Looking at precisely operate the true gift from God, unknown language as speaking in tongues.

Tongues Edify a Person:
The Word clearly says that he who speaks in tongues will speak an unknown language. He begins to worship directly to the Lord Jesus. No one can understand the heavenly language except the Holy Spirit.

Only He can understand the language which He gave as a gift to the individual. Although this experience, we speak in an unknown language, and we don't even understand ourselves.

It brings a significant spiritual uplifting to every Christian life. A person who speaks in a tongue builds up himself. He lifts himself on a high level of Spiritual holiness.

As we also know that he who speaks in tongue would increase, and it will strengthen and edifies himself.

"He who speaks in a tongue edifies himself." 1 Corinthians 14:4, NKJV.

Edify the church:
There is always an excellent gift that would bring to the church. Today we see there is a lack of having a word of prophecy in many churches. The Lord loves to speak to His church, and we must remember the church belongs to Jesus.

If there is someone who has a call of God to give a word of prophecy, the church would recognize it and let him speak to edify the church. The one who prophesies has a privilege to bring a message from God to the congregation.

The Lord will choose the one who is anointed to the gift of prophecy. And the Lord will choose someone else to interpret, so that it may edify the whole congregation. We read the Word uses for this is "edification."

It means the one who will be used to bring the word of prophecy to the church to builds up the spiritual growth in 'knowledge, loyalty, happiness, righteousness.' The main purpose of spiritual gifts is to build up the body of Christ.

"he who prophesies edifies the church." 1 Corinthians 14:4, NKJV.

Praising with New Language:

We are praising God with the language which pleasing unto Him. Our spirit will have a spirit of God to join with Him. That's why we receive a gift of a new language to glorify His name.

Even Satan cannot understand it. When we receive the baptism of the Spirit by lays hands on us, we receive a few words that would come out of our mouth.

Then we start speaking and singing with a few words. We continue praising Him until a few words will increase too many words. It's a remarkable experience that we will be able to praise and worshipping the Lord.

The Lord formed it for the church. Every Christian believer can receive a free gift. Some will not accept the gift because of not believing the baptism in the Holy Spirit. But some believers are hungry to get more of the Lord.

They are ready to get empowerment by the Spirit of God. This new language will help us to grow in a spiritual walk with the Lord. It will strengthen our spiritual gifts in the ministry.

Especially a new language of the Holy Spirit will help a preacher or minister of the Gospel to get direction on how to make right a decision in life and ministry.

Activate Our Gifts:
Praying in tongues will release the anointing of God to activate our gifts, along with the fruit of the Spirit. Each servant or a preacher would have a good fruit of the spirit to be an example of the Lord.

It's vital to have every spiritual gift to build up in us to grow into effectiveness. Praying in tongues helps us to become strong in our spiritual life, to fulfill God's plan. He has predestined us to a great purpose to fulfill the call of God.

We desire to be a servant and to be a witness for the Lord and preaching the authoritative Word of God. When we operate those nine gifts of the spirit with the compassion of Jesus, wisdom, and purity, they are an essential achievement of the ministry.

Relationship with The Word:
The relationship with the Word is significant, more than anything else. It is very vital to learn that the gifts of the spirit are a loving

relationship with the Lord. This is the reason to have intimacy with the Word; we will make it in life and ministry.

We must remember, we will never serve completely in the gifts of the spirit, without experiencing the Word of God.

We must be active in the fire of prayer life. It will release the impartation of the anointing of God through our relationship with the Word. We need to take in the Word into our hearts to meditate and decree the works of God.

If the Lord instructs us to do something or tell us to obey Him, it should be line-up with scripture. He will speak to us, and He will be able to confirm it by His Word.

Interpret the Message:
We have seen in many places which the Fellowship gathered for the service with many spirits-filled believers. These people were trying to worship the Lord Jesus by speaking in tongues altogether.

I have seen in the middle of worship service when the church becomes silent. The Holy Spirit impresses a person to speak with prophecy words, giving encouraging messages to the church.

It means the person speaks in tongues; the Lord will choose some else to interpret the unknown language to the assembly. Here, someone is selected by the Holy Spirit for the church in which he delivers the message of prophecy to the people for understanding the language.

Paul instructs the church in those events. If there is someone who has the spiritual ability to interpret the message, the church should recognize it.

In this way, the whole body of believers will understand the language and get a blessing by the message.

"I wish you all spoke with tongues, but even more that you prophesied; for he who prophesies is greater than he who speaks with tongues, unless indeed he interprets, that *the church may receive edification.*" 1 Corinthians 14:5, NKJV.

A True Baptism:

True baptism is leading us to better dynamic work of His leadership and His presence in our daily lifestyles. He is able to make awareness in all circumstances and our ministry's situations, families, to make the right decision for us. To allow the influence of the Lord in our daily activities could be useful.

We can have full confidence in our preaching with the fullness of His power. It will be a real baptism because He will empower us into His Glory. He will direct us when we don't know where we go! But we trust in His name, and we have His real baptism in us to walk under His protection.

We must be a genuine person to receive all His gifts. We need Him to create a clean and humble heart for us that we can be connected to the true baptism. We really want to be that kind person with a pure character in Christ.

A real baptism would take place in the life of every person. It must be received with excitement then will change the person's life forever.

Intercessory Prayer:
Intercessor person who intercedes on behalf of another. An intercessor person who called by the Lord to walk on fire. The Lord has called a few believers to become an intercessory prayer

for other people. We must remember that not everyone can do the intercessory prayer.

Prayer warriors are pushing forward in spiritual warfare against enemies. The prayer warriors are standing in the middle of a crisis to ask God to demolish the enemy territory. An intercessory prayer would be living on fire. It will bring more healing, and miracles of the Lord would happen. There should be a message of the Gospel preached to lost souls.

Seeking God to pray for an individual or a large group, it needs to hear the Spirit what He wants or how He wants to pray! Jesus gave a desire to many who wish to be used as an intercessory prayer warrior. It's always the people who need help will go to victory.

It usually needs intercessory prayer to support friends and family through crises. We may perform intercessory prayer on behalf of someone dealing with a dangerous breakdown. It may operate prayer to serve and save someone's life or families.

God's servants must recognize the power and hearing the voice of God. The Lord makes a beautiful relationship with His servants, who would have the heart to obey the Word of God.

The Lord will train His own leaders and servants of God. He helps His preacher to be on Fire, and he must be willing to come to His presence. The Lord will anoint His servants to preach, how to pray, and how to sing of praise and worship.

The spirit of 'intercessory prayer' doesn't give up. It's the love of prayer that holds us strong in all difficulties and conquers every hindrance. It's our worship and praise that 'pushes forward' to defeat the giant mountain.

We are experiencing; it's God's power that will allow any conditions in life that will lead to triumph. He is able to fulfill our desire to take us into the heavenly presence of God.

Intercession:
Intercession means getting a grip of God's power and denying our flash to let go until His Fire would come down. Intercession is a prayer that our needs move up to the Lord, and He is the One who makes way for us. We know there are a lot of needs out there to intercede for others.

Intercession is warfare; when we enter into the prayer warzone, we are going into spiritual warfare. The sign is to recognize that it is not our battle, but it's God's battle. We trust in His strategy to fight the battle for our lives.

We pray and praise His name; He prepares the battleground to win any attack of the enemy. We walk by faith with no fear and no panic, let Him prepare the way of victory for us. There will always be a need for prayer everywhere around us.

Living with the love of God produces *the Fire of God*. Then we hear, there is an urgent prayer for a family member who is suffering a terrible sickness. Or our friends or neighbor desperately needs a touch of God's love.

In this kind of situation, we respond very quickly to go into intercession that the Lord heals and brings restoration to the families. The peace of the Lord to save others.

The reward of the Lord will come back to us later. At the same time, we share the salvation of the Lord to those who need the peace of God. We see everywhere from across nations, communities, families, and everything rises to deteriorate every life.

We realize because these people control their own faith, worshipping in other gods. God gave us a free choice, what to believe, or what kind of god to follow. Usually, the problems would occur; then, we experience a heavy burden on us to carry.

We believe our God is bigger than any obstacle. If we want to fix our troubles with our own power, there is no effect on our intercession. We intercede even though we know we cannot deal with them on our ability.

But the Lord is our solve-maker. It's moments like these circumstances when we call for every 'Prayer Warrior' to pray in one accord altogether. Our intercession should be bringing an impossible situation to turn around to victory by God's warrior angels in heaven.

• CHAPTER 11 •

The Fire of God and Prayer

IF WE DON'T LOVE the Lord Jesus, we cannot read His Word, and we cannot even really pray in the name of the Lord. Therefore, it must be love, faith, and belief that He is here in the midst of our prayer time.

We love Jesus because He loved us first. The Bible says God the Father gave His only begotten Son for our sins to bring us back to Himself to love us and to give us hope and everlasting life. We enter into prayer time when we believe that we love Him, and we follow Him for the rest of our lives because He is the God of love.

The Word said: He gave us faith to believe that He is a God of love, and He is a master of love, and the nature of God is holy and love.

"So then faith comes by hearing, and hearing by the word of God." Romans 10:17, NKJV.

Having a Desire for Prayer:
There is a desire in everyone's life to draw into prayer and learn about God. There should be a love for prayer that we recognize that our love for Jesus draws us near to the Holy Spirit to bring us closer to the Word of God.

Anytime I get down on my knees and begin to pray with my Jewish Tallit to cover myself. I feel His love there, and He is waiting for me to talk to Him. I see Him in my spirit, and I need to express my gratitude to Him.

When we are close to the Word of God, the Holy Spirit will bring all knowledge about God into our mind and soul. Our love for the Lord should grow and become strong, as the Holy Spirit will give us a revelation of Jesus's love for us.

He loves us and gives us peace and heals our hearts to bring a fresh change. The Bible says: The Lord is transforming us from glory to glory.

"But we all, with unveiled face, beholding as in a mirror the glory of the Lord, are being

transformed into the same image from glory to glory, just as by the Spirit of the Lord." 1 Corinthians 10:31, NKJV.

Love His Presence:
I just wanted to remind you. If there is no Fire of God, there will not be the presence of His Glory; it will be an empty atmosphere. If we don't honor the Lord Jesus, we cannot study the Word, and not even having intimacy with the Lord.

There must be faith, love, and confidence that He is standing in the midst of our prayer. The Bible said we must carry our cross daily and love Him with the whole heart and mind and strength. We worship Jesus because He loved us first.

The Bible says God the Father gave His only begotten Son for our sins to bring us back to Himself to love us and to give us hope and everlasting life.

We enter into prayer time when we believe that we love Him. We follow Him for the rest of our lives because He is the God of love. He gave us faith to believe, and He is a master of love, and the nature of God is holy and love.

He Ministers with the Fire:
The Lord is always ministering to us in unique ways, even though we don't pay attention to His signs. He is watching over us because of His power and glory. He loves to minister to us every day—not only that, but He is leading into His Fire in every moment of our lives.

He is revealing His greatness and His sovereignty to us. He wants to be in charge of every aspect of our lives.

"For He shall give His angels charge over you, To keep you in all your ways." Psalm 91:11, NKJV.

Serving with His Fire:
We need to ask Him, "Would you please take control of my life?" Then we need to rest in Him and have peace in ourselves. The Lord is often waiting for us to walk with Him, and He covers us and takes care of our lives. Loving the Lord in our daily life is sometimes challenging with the attack of the enemy; it can be very complicated.

We go through temptation and trial of life, and sometimes we forget the Lord. He wants us to minister unto Him in prayer with love.

In fact, He is serving us with His Fire, and remember His Fire is His presence. He is an excellent servant. He said, "I came to serve, not to be served." Praise His Holy Name.

"For even the Son of Man did not come to be served, but to serve, and to give His life a ransom for many." Mark 10:45, NKJV.

God's Voice in the Fire:
The Lord is transforming us and changing us in the spiritual realm to be able to discern God's voice. The Holy Spirit is genuinely faithful to teach us a perfect way to lead us and guide us in the spiritual plan of God. The Holy Spirit will never lead us in the wrong direction. He knows how to speak to us.

Becoming hungry for Him to hear His sweet voice, it's required spending time in His Word and His presence. Try to read His Word, and soaking in His presence. Seek Him to know Him better. He is a loving Father who has a warm voice.

As we know that the devil is a liar, and he cannot do anything to us; he is continually trying to deceive us in many ways. We can defeat him by the Word of God and ignore him; he cannot control our minds anymore. We decree the blood of Jesus and pleading the blood of the Lamb over us.

Speak loud in your prayer and cleanse yourself under the blood of Jesus every day. Then you will hear His voice clearly, and you will become hungry for Him and come into His presence to hear His voice.

Can We Hear God's Voice?

I would say: Yes. We can hear Him, and He is always ready to speak to us in prayer. In fact, He has communicated to us through His Word. When we read His Word, this is His voice. He spoke at the beginning of the creation of the human being.

Some people would recognize His voice, and some Christians cannot hear Him. It depends on how we grow up in Christian life, and if we always train ourselves to acknowledge Him at all times. We must teach ourselves in intercession and seek His face and pursue His Word to get answers and hear His beautiful voice.

• CHAPTER 12 •

Relationship with the Fire

THE BAPTISM OF THE Holy Spirit can lead us to a beautiful relationship with the Lord. We meet many new believers in Christ, and they receive the baptism in the Holy Spirit. Their lives get changed and to transfer the way of the Christian life.

A new believer would receive an excitement of new life in Christ with a good heart and with a passionate love to reach out to lost souls. Because of having a fresh experience in the mighty Spirit of God. A new believer would have to speak an unknown language which will get after getting baptized.

There will be a few words we received during the time our baptism in the Holy Spirit.

Remember a few words that can increase to many words because the Lord will multiply more words to our prayers with new tongues.

As a new believer, our relationship with the Lord becomes stronger after the baptism. In fact, we become hungry and thirsty for His direction and His love.

Asking for the Fire:

The whole world is searching for the fire and the presence of God. We live in an exciting time. The people are from every nation are pursuing the love of God. Everyone is looking to live in peace, joy, and hope in Christ.

We are all looking for the power of God that will separate us from every darkness's spirit. The Fire would burn every sickness to bring healing and deliverance. God wishes to give us the desire of our hearts.

Asking God for His fire, when we seek Him in prayer, He will grant it to us. Without the fire of God, we experience, we are out of power. Without real-life, we will not fulfill our destiny. Without enthusiasm, we become empty inside-out.

Without the fire of God, we will have only theology or Christian doctrine, or knowledge that what we've learned from the Bible. Usually, we would like to study the Word first; later, He changes us into Godly life.

But if we allow ourselves into a vessel of honor. He will make a significant result in a beautiful relationship with the Holy Spirit. We ask Him in prayer for a mighty move of His presence that we can change ourselves. Then we can serve and pray for healing.

Fire Cleanses Us:
We will ask the Lord to cleanse us from all unrighteousness. And the Lord is revealing in His Word, to purify ourselves under His Word, and let His Word sanctify us. He still requires us to decree the blood of the Lamb of God.

First, we will seek the Holy Spirit to reveal to us where are our impurities or sins in our lives. We're praying *the Fire* will burn all our sins, sickness, and then bringing purification and sanctification of the spirit.

Fire takes away our form of wrong activity. Fire overcomes the failure. Fire consumes the sinful character, and He cleanses us with His blood. Jesus can cover us with His loving heart.

The time of the outpouring of fire from the Holy Spirit falls on every person to make a clean heart. The fire of God will ready to restore, whom God chose to use in His Kingdom. Another work of God's fire is wiping out every person's obstacle.

Purity in the Fire:
We will grow to the highest level of maturity to become very easy to come into His presence in worship. We feel we are free from sins, and there is no sense of guilt or condemnation in our spirit anymore. We have peace in ourselves and intimacy with the Lord. The Lord will be pleased, and we desire to stay pure in His Fire and holy before the Lord.

The better we work with the Holy Spirit to have a pure heart, the stronger we become in the power of His might. We experience that if we allow seeds of sins to grow called: "sin's seed" on the ground.

After a while, we will continue to commit sins again. It means that we give water to "sin's seed," and the seed begins to take root, and eventually, the time appears when we reap a terrible harvest.

The result will be spiritual blindness; we will become prideful and deny the truth of the Word of God. We won't see a clear manifestation of the purity of ourselves in our prayer. The harvest can bring sickness; it will bring a crisis in the family or at the job or cause us to be involved in an accident.

Anything can happen when the time of harvest comes; the seed will produce the unwanted harvest. And the Lord is revealing in His Word, to purify ourselves by His Fire, and let His Word sanctify us. He also wants us to declare that the blood of the Lamb of God will purify us.

First, we will ask the Holy Spirit to reveal to us, where are our impurities or sins. We're praying for purification and sanctification of the spirit. The pure heart is vital in worship, and it sets apart sanctification from sin. It is vital to have a purity to draw us into the presence of the Lord.

Another reason the Bible is telling us is to set ourselves apart from the evil spirit; dedicate ourselves unto the Lord. It means that we can stay away from all sins around us, and we don't need to be a part of the lies of the enemy.

It is easy to have eyes blinded and be completely naive in spiritual prayer life. And the devil is deceiving us with all his accusations. When the time of temptation appears to attack us, we can say no to the impurity of sins.

"For this is the will of God, your sanctification: that you should abstain from sexual immorality; that each of you should know how to possess his own vessel in sanctification and honor." 1 Thessalonians 4:3-4, NKJV.

Set Our Hearts on Fire:
Allowing our hearts will have a longing after His Fire. He will set us into the anointing of His presence. He will lead and guide us into a beautiful future. Let His truthfulness and His Spirit motivate us. He will be equipping us with an understanding of the marvelous things. He chooses us to make us like Himself.

Let's all get on fire for God by sincerely praying and patiently. We are earnestly studying His Word, we will let His truth, and His Spirit touch us. We all have a great ambition to get saturated with the supernatural vision.

We know many great things will come to pass; we need to obey His Word daily. He goes before us and to make us strong in His Fire. He makes signs and wonders through us. And let us do our part by setting our full heart into a new assignment we can do for Jesus and others.

New Stage of Fire:
To become a dynamic preacher, I would say it's needed to be a prayer warrior. The prayer will get us into the spirit of passion and building up a desire to be used by Him. Making ourselves available and tell Him, *"Lord, here I am; use me."* He is taking us to an unknown place to be a witness of the Lord Jesus.

God wants to deliver people from the bondage of darkness into the light and heal a broken heart. The fire of God brings glorious miracles for His honor. We desire to step up to a new level of authority so that we can rebuke the devil for removing him from any crisis or sickness from a Christian home.

Today, many faithful Christian believers are very dedicated to attending the church to serve any place in the Body of Christ. But on the other hand, they're suffering in their problems, especially in sickness. All they do is to continue going to the doctor and the hospital to get recovered.

It is God's will to get healed. We shall step up in faith, stand up in the gap for others, and intercede for the saints of God. I think it is an excellent thing to put our faith in action for serving others in prayer.

We move up into the spirit of maturity to pray for other believers around us. He gives us a fresh anointing on us to know His direction where He is taking us to a new level of fire.

Fire in Prayer Life:

The fire of God is burning all the sickness and problems in those faithful believers. Examine your prayer life if you feel that your prayer does not get through in the fire. If it is not allowing you to move up to the next level of spiritual maturity, and perhaps it needs more anointing of the Holy Spirit.

If we feel when we pray that our hearts are empty, make sure that we are seeking God in our best. We are pressing forward to the fire of the Spirit. I encourage you to ask the Holy Spirit to fire you up. Try to praise Him with worship music, praying, and reading the Word at the same time.

If you are not baptized in the Holy Spirit, you probably need to get baptized soon. I mentioned before in the other chapter. Because when the Holy Spirit comes on you. You receive power and the fire of the Holy Spirit to empower you to witness.

You can then pray with an unknown language of the Spirit for yourself and minister to someone by the boldness and authority of God.

I believe that the Lord is there with me and hearing me. I love the fire of the Holy Spirit that moves upon me to make me a winner. I love to impact my fresh anointing to release the fire of God on other people. I would like to minister to many with a word of knowledge, and a word of wisdom called the "prophetic word."

"But he who prophesies speaks edification and exhortation and comfort to men." 1 Corinthians 14:3, NKJV.

Set Our Hearts on Fire:
Let's put Jesus in the center of our hearts; let us set Him up in a higher throne in heaven. Our deeper intensity can move us in Spiritual submission under the Fire of the Lord. He will lead us into many marvelous plans. We allow Him to set our hearts on fire, and we desire to achieve many tasks.

It requires focusing on Jesus and put Him in front, to be in the center in every worship and ministry. Get ready to place Jesus into heart and life altogether. We walk in the spirit, and we must walk humbly under His authority.

When we acknowledge Him in all circumstances, he will release His Fire, and His presence will consume all our sinful desires from us. We need to get free from ourselves, becoming a humble servant and a great preacher on Fire.

Setting our love on fire and set His Glory into our path. Let His joy be our passion through His presence. God's will shall be ours; it will allow us to join with His kindness.

We fail, but we rise again, and we expect He shall answer all of our prayer requests. We desire to have a real character, dedication, and heart expectation. We're expecting a beautiful thing from our lovely Father.

We experience our Father's Word, and His promise is true. He is not leading us to the wrong path of promise. He set our hearts in the right direction. Amen.

Let Your Fire Fall:
Be cheerful always to receive the Fire of God, to fall down on us from His presence. We will lift up His name higher in our worship and praise. We raise up our voice to worship and glorify His name. Praying in the fire makes a difference.

We have an expectation of prayer in our daily prayers. When we have devotion, we expect to hear Him; we discover His voice. He gives us visions and dreams to open our hearts to Him. He will wait for us to show us which way we have to go or to teach us which person we must to minister and to serve.

God is expecting us to have faith, and He requires us to believe His Word. He promises to love us and cares for us to answer us in this confusing world. Praying without expectation changes nothing. We must identify what God spoke in His Word that the Fire is falling down upon every spirit-filled.

God performed His Fire for us by the supernatural power of His Glory. The falling of His Fire is very easy to take us to higher glory. The Fire breaks down a complicated life and crisis to upside down to the new life. We look at the people are striving to get to the promised land of blessing.

Every journey of life is complex to survive. But when God makes promises to us from the beginning of our journey in walking with Him. He will be responsible for taking us to the end of the journey.

A Passionate Person:
It is stating that a passionate person desires to go into a deep commitment and living with the Fire of God. Serving and preaching the Word is opening up a new encounter with people into

their life. Specially, we must set ourselves as an example of a humble servant. The Lord wants us to live with purity to receive more of His anointing.

A passionate person is dedicated to stand up and get ready to pray. Then he will accomplish the impossible task of the Kingdom of God. A servant of God is working hard work for the sake of others to pray and to intercede for saving and healing others.

A preacher of the Gospel is focused on the direction and the plan of God. It's needed the leadership of the Holy Spirit to receive the visions and the dreams from the Lord. A servant of God is willing to go extra miles for others to lie down his life for serving other believers and nonbelievers.

Prayer Warriors in the Fire:
As a spirit-filled believer in the Lord, we are called to become a prayer warrior. We must recognize the Spirit of Lord, who has full control of our prayer. The Lord wants to confirm to us the breakthrough belongs to a prayer warrior.

Let Jesus know, "Lord, I need Fire in my prayer to get a breakthrough." But if something is not right in the Holy Spirit. He is revealing to us, so we will humble ourselves before His presence to perform a significant breakthrough.

I believe we deserve a breakthrough if we are committed to seeking His face and spending time in the Word. He is pouring out His Glory on us. We trust Him in all His ways.

As a preacher must have a heart of prayer, without prayer cannot get the victory through spiritual warfare. When the Fire comes down on God's anointed preacher to do an impossible task. He will surprise us to make supernatural phenomena for the Glory of God.

As a man of God becomes more humble in prayer to hear His voice. The only way, the Glory will come down through seeking Him. A preacher needs to see vision and dream for the people of God and other nations.

Rest in His Presence:
Let's look upon Jesus and know that He is surrounding us with His tenderness and love. He sees the cry of our hearts. Now it is time to rest

in His presence. We do our part in worship and give our heavy burden unto Him. He is accomplishing His part. The powerful thing is that He is covering us with an extraordinarily caring spirit.

We rest in Him and lay down our thoughts, our pains, our worries, and our fears in Him. We desire to get peace in ourselves and leave all other matters in God's hand.

I want to mention here about having confidence in His Word, resting and trusting in His Might presence. He will bring His magnificent of His Fire to pour out on us because of our faith in Him.

When we are leaning on His ability, he is able to protect us with all His power, His glory. So, there will not be any evil spirit or sickness near to us. There is no fear in us, and He has cast away all enemies for protecting His people.

As a preacher who is serving, it needs to relax in the peace of God, which would be very significant. Let the Lord fight your battle; you can't do anything by your own strength; it doesn't work.

When we get tired and start sitting down, maybe it is the time to surrender our anxiety to the Lord. We fight in ourselves and compete with others or struggling in some situations that need to be fixed. But if it still doesn't work, we can start to make peace in ourselves and rest in the Lord.

I have seen many servants of God included many different missionaries and those who are serving, which going to Evangelism. They love God, having a great desire to serve with the whole heart, mind, and soul to serve.

But there is fear that will hinder them; it will stop them from moving forward. It will only need to go deep in the Fire of God. That all fear and worry shall go away, In Jesus' name. Amen.

Heavenly Touch:
One-touch changes everything and brings a new life. Just one "heavenly touch" from His presence can transform every obstacle in daily life. It will remove one thing at a time that we are striving with difficulty. He is touching us with His mighty Fire from heaven.

I believe every minister of God will go through the challenge of ministry, health, family, finance, or other things in life. One-touch from His presence would change everything. We need to burn every obstacle, and He leads us into Glorious victory.

Our Father will touch us from His throne. He will anoint His preacher, ordinary servants in the church. He prepares those who have chosen to testify His Mighty Words.

Sometimes, we need to receive His Fire and His anointing, but it needs to spend a lot of time in reading His Words and prayer. Desiring to go *Fasting* will humble us know Him more into experiencing His love.

Hearing His Voice:

Let's talk about the manifestation of God's voice in the Fire. Can we hear God's voice? I would say yes. We can hear Him, and He is always ready to speak to us in prayer. In fact, He has reached out to us through His Word. When we read His Word, this is His voice. He spoke at the beginning of creation.

Some people would recognize His voice, and some Christians cannot hear Him. It depends on how we grow up in the Christian life. But if we train ourselves to identify Him in the Fire, which is His presence.

We must discipline ourselves in intercession prayer and seek His face. Today we as a minister of the Gospel must pursue His Word to get answers and hearing His beautiful voice. The Holy Spirit is very faithful to show us the right way to lead us and guide us in the divine plan of God. The Holy Spirit will never talk to us in the wrong way, and He knows how to speak to us.

As a preacher must live on the Fire of God and be able to talk loud in his prayer. We will cleanse ourselves under the blood of Jesus every day. Then we will hear His voice clearly, and we will become thirsty for Him.

We are coming into His presence to discern His voice. To become hungry for hearing Him requires reading His Word, listening, and meditating in His presence. Seek Him to experience Him better. He is a loving Father who has a warm voice.

Rejoice in the Fire:
Preaching the Word without the joy of the Lord would make us very heavy in the spirit. Can we

rejoice in the Lord all the time? We are living in a world that is full of chaos and confusion from every situation of daily disorder of lifestyle.

Some people would say; it's hard to rejoice in the Lord and to be a witness of Christ at the same time! They're also saying when we come to pray without joy, which we had gladness in our daily activities. We cannot find anything because the world took all our joy away through our job and our family.

We desire to move forward, to get our joy back, and to get our peace of the Lord to enter the gates of praise and worship. Rejoicing in the Lord is extremely powerful, and having comfort in prayer. We celebrate Him in worship because we depend on His Word; we trust in His presence.

He is alive and is here with us. We are not alone by ourselves; He is anointing us to rejoice in His salvation and rejoice in His love. He is dealing with all our problems and resolving our chaos at work or in the family.

He has established our faith through His Word and our new life in Him by the anointing of joy. The Bible would say; the Lord is rejoicing in the presence of His angels for one soul who would be found into the Kingdom of God.

When a person gives his life back to God, the Almighty God shall rejoice for many lost souls found. Having faith and trust would create joy and hope that will take place in the presence of the Lord.

Some Christians ministers are becoming lukewarm in faith because they are not experiencing joy in prayer. They prayed for healing, or they asked for their situation to be resolved. But they didn't receive an answer to their prayer.

They broke down, and the devil tried to take them away from the Lord. The devil stole their joy because they became angry and frustrated, not continuing by faith in the Word. Remember, He is faithful. He is good.

• CHAPTER 13 •

Jesus Calls Us to the Ministry

I MEAN, HE CALLS us to the ministry, He can stir our spirit into new fresh preaching. The Lord called many Christians to a different ministry to preparing them to be sent out. It is necessary first to check our hearts and desire.

Every person carries an extraordinary calling from the Lord. He has invited us into His salvation and to grow in spiritual maturity. He calls us to an amazing way of His Kingdom to love and serve others. However, some are called in the public service highly respected.

The Lord Jesus invites lost souls to himself to save them. As we know, His love is that all people get served. So, if we're a believer, we are called! Surely, there is a call upon every believer that sets a specific task for men or women in the church.

The New Testament indicates to some given as 'Apostles, Prophets, Evangelists, Pastors, and Teachers.' And they've given to the congregation. Some given to plant a church. Some given to prophecy.

Some given to teach the Word of God. Some given to preach the message of the Gospel. Some given to be a shepherd for the flock of the body of Christ. Some given to equip Christian believers. Some given an anointing to mentor those who are called to walk on the fire of God.

I would like to share from one of my previous books, which I wrote about the five-fold ministry.

Apostles:
The title of "Apostle" is a true call of God to serve as Christ, who is head of the Church. It's an honor to become an ambassador of Christ as a missionary to all nations to establish the congregation for the Lord Jesus.

Basically, planting a church in a local city and all countries around the world. Also, it's called to oversee the church of Christ, which has established already. An apostle would help to plant a new Fellowship and build up the Church on the Word of God.

An Apostle can determine to select God's leader for the local church. It means the Holy Spirit will instruct His servant to choose the right spirit-filled leader. The primary task of Apostle to make sure the Godly leader is living in purity for serving the saint of God.

The teaching is correct in Biblical doctrine, which must be preached from the true Word of God. To make sure there are no false theological trends and no wrong teaching in the Church of God.

Prophets:
The title of "Prophets" is a person who delivers a message of God by divine inspiration of the Holy Spirit to encourage and to predict the future in the church. The main concern of the servant is the spiritual life and purity of the church.

"having been built on the foundation of the apostles and prophets, Jesus Christ Himself

being the chief cornerstone."** Ephesians 2:20, NKJV.

The Prophet will have functioned under the anointing of the Holy Spirit to interpret the word of God called to warn, to exhort, to comfort, and to edify the Body of Christ:

"But he who prophesies speaks edification and exhortation and comfort to men. 4 He who speaks in a tongue edifies himself, but he who prophesies edifies the church." 1 Corinthians 14:3-4 NKJV.

The Prophet is called to expose the sin, to proclaim the righteousness of God, to warn of judgment may take place. To oppose worldliness, to inform about Luke warmness and accepting beliefs that contradict the faith.

The message will be a warning for false teaching. Must the church discern and test the message of Prophet to be true or not? The Prophet will be accountable to his message, and his words must be delivered directly from God.

Evangelists:

The title of "Evangelists" is called to preach the "Good News" of the Gospel to lost souls. The message of Salvation will be preached throughout the world. The Evangelist must be full of anointing of the Holy Spirit and have a passion for lost people.

The church would have to establish the ministry of Evangelists to reach unreached people in the city. The Evangelist is fundamental to God's purpose for the church. The message of Evangelist brings a new convert and allows the church to grow and train more evangelists.

"Then Philip opened his mouth, and beginning at this Scripture, preached Jesus to him." Acts 8:35, NKJV.

It leads us to a clear perception of the work of an evangelist. It's said, Philip, the Evangelist, preached the Good News of the Salvation. Many people got saved and baptized with water, special signs and wonders, and healings took place.

New believer gave their lives, and they filled with the Holy Spirit. These new converts added to the congregation. This is the way the church should grow by allowing a Gift of ministry to operate in the Body of Christ to work of the ministry.

Pastors:

The title of "Pastors" is called to be a shepherd of the flock in the church. Pastors are those who oversee and seeking for special care for the needs of their people in the congregation. Their task to preach and teach with the sound doctrine. Pastors' responsibility for watching out for any false teaching and wrong Bible doctrine for their flocks in the church.

"Shepherd the flock of God which is among you, serving as overseers, not by compulsion but willingly, not for dishonest gain but eagerly." 1 Peter 5:2 NKJV.

The church should appoint godly pastors to look after their members and provide them with spiritual food. The pastor would have to bring other spiritual encouragement needed for growth in a healthy relationship with Christ. They should feed their congregation's hunger with the words of faith and discipline the flock in godliness.

Teachers:

The title of "Teachers" is called to teach the truth of the Word of God and nothing else. They are fundamental to God's purpose for his church to build up the flocks' faith, which is needed to become strong in their salvation. The main task of teachers is to guide by the leadership of the Holy Spirit. The Lord has entrusted to them to speak the truth of the eternal Word of Almighty God to the Body of Christ.

"For this reason I also suffer these things; nevertheless, I am not ashamed, for I know whom I have believed and am persuaded that He is able to keep what I have committed to Him until that Day." 2 Tim 1:12 NKJV.

The primary purpose of Biblical teaching is to protect the integrity and to present holiness by serving Christ's body. Having a true responsibility to the godly lifestyle in God's Word. God's inspired Word will come to the final test of all learning and teaching. The congregation will be continually emphasizing that the inspired Word of God is absolutely truthful and is full of authority.

• CHAPTER 14 •

How I received the Fire of God

I LOVE TO SHARE my experience with you, how I started walking on the Fire of God in my Christian life. I had a good experience in my entire spiritual life with the Lord. Everyone will go through the challenge of living with families or sickness and any other crisis. It may be natural for everybody.

So, this is my testimony to how I got saved by the Grace of God. And How I received the Fire of God.

My Testimony:
When I was 24, I realized that something was missing in my life that no one could help me. Nobody could understand my heart. I tried to be

a good person, and I sought to be able to survive in my own way. I wanted to find the truth of life.

My question was: where am I coming from? What is the purpose of life? I had no faith or not believing in God. I knew there must be something up there more than my life. I needed peace and joy and finding the meaning of life.

I was living an ordinary life with no destiny and future. I began seeking and researching many different ways to find the truth. I tried to hang out with some friends for entertainment to really finding joy. Sometimes I had to use alcohol and drug to have fun and forget my pain in life.

The more I began searching for the truth, the more I became thirsty for peace of God. I needed to find the true God who created me. I couldn't see, God was really looking after my life even though I didn't have a relationship with Him.

So, in December 1984, God brought someone into my life who was a born-again Christian. He was living on fire for God that he shared a message of the Gospel to me. He witnessed to me and explained in an easy way that only Jesus gives everything that I need in my life.

The time I met him in the winter season of the Christmas holiday 1984. He approached me and offered me a small New Testament. I have never had a bible before. It was the first time someone came to me with the Word of God.

I said to myself, maybe I need to read this book; I have nothing to lose. It is my choice to accept the truth or not! So, I began reading the only four books of the Gospel in the New Testament. I couldn't understand the Word, not a lot, but I could feel His presence in my heart.

I loved reading many beautiful stories, miracles, and healing of Jesus. The Holy Spirit started to reveal the Word to me. Every time I read the Word, I could see my sins that I am a sinner.

I wondered why there are some stories of Jesus in four similar Gospels. I could see myself in the Word, which the Word was as a mirror that I am not right with God. Jesus paid the price in my place. He died on the cross for me; I might have a new life.

The Word gave lots of spiritual understanding about how to get changed and start a new life in Christ. I tried other things to change, but it didn't work out. I wanted really to be transformed inside-out in the Lord Jesus. He revealed His Word to me that He is my creator. He is my destiny and my eternal life.

So, I made the right choice coming in God's presence on January 15, 1985. That night I was alone all by myself in my room. I have decided to do something in my life and for my future.

I took the New Testament in my hand; I felt that the Word is my only hope of life. I kneeled down and put the small New Testament on my face and cried out to the Lord for mercy. I didn't know how to talk to God or how to pray! And how to express my need to Him.

I said: Oh God; I don't know you are up there or not? I need you to help me to believe in you and to reveal Jesus to me. I cried with a repent heart for a while until the Holy Spirit brought understanding that Jesus is the only savior of my life.

I prayed: Jesus, you are the Son of God, Jesus come into my life and my heart, be my Lord and my Savior forever. I asked Jesus to forgive all my sins and cleanse me and making me a new person inside.

I made a great covenant with the Lord, and I promised to serve Him for the rest of my life. That night I went to sleep. I woke up the next day. I could feel a sense of peace and had no desire for alcohol or drug anymore.

I could see my heart, and my life began to transform every day. I started to share my testimony to others, what the Lord Jesus has done for me. Because Jesus has changed my life for the Glory of God.

I realized that I needed to share the Word to those who have not heard the good news of the Gospel yet. Then after I got saved, I joined a Pentecostal church in Copenhagen, Denmark. I wanted to serve Him and to serve God's people.

I sought the Lord about my call on how to fulfill it. After three years later, I involved in the Youth Outreach ministry. The Lord has spoken to me directly, and He called me to serve Him as a minister of the Gospel in His Kingdom.

I believe it is a great honor to become a servant of Jesus. After 35 years in Christ, I am still serving Him and rejoicing in His grace every day. Glory to His name. Jesus is Lord.

Receiving Baptism in the Water:

I continued going to the Pentecostal church and learning the Word of God. After a couple of months later. One Sunday, after church service, they shared with me that I can get a baptism immersion in water.

They explained to me that it is the right thing to get water baptized. They told me it is the biblical truth to go underwater. It was then coming out of the water that it is written in the book of Romans 6: 4, NKJV.

"Therefore we were buried with Him through baptism into death, that just as Christ was raised from the dead by the glory of the Father, even so we also should walk in newness of life."

As a new believer, we must be buried with Jesus through baptism into death. I was fulfilling the Word of God concerning the baptism in water.

Receiving Baptism in the Spirit:

Later on, a month later, I was in the meeting with Christian members of the church. They were talking about baptism in the Holy Spirit.

I didn't know there was another baptism in the Bible. I heard carefully; I was so excited to experience more about the Fire of the Holy Spirit.

I had such a hunger to learn about the Holy Spirit. They shared with me that I will receive the empowerment of the Holy Spirit to use for my personal life and ministry. They laid hands on me and praying in the Holy Spirit.

Suddenly, I cried in my spirit; I could see the Lord is pouring down His power on me with a new language. I was speaking with a few words. Then I asked them, how can I know that I am baptized. They said it's a sign that you speak with other tongues.

The Spirit will give a few words and fill you up with power from heaven. Then you will worship and praise the Lord Jesus with a new language. Daily pray will help with a few words become more word to praying in the spirit.

Dwell in the Fire of God

I realize every Christian believer would have a great desire to live and walking in the Fire of God. Some believers would love to get more Fire, and some get less Fire. It depends on the person's desire, which will lead us to have more of God.

When I received a call from God to preach, I had a passion for Street Evangelism to reach out to lost souls. At the same time, some members of my church had another assignment from the Lord. They will do an excellent job in the church. I had such love to share the Gospel with lost souls.

I still have the desire to preach the Good News of the Lord Jesus. We need to look at what we have received, a call from the Lord. Some are good in many different areas of the ministry, but they are not effective in Street Evangelism.

But they are valuable in the heart of God that He is using them in the area He wants them to serve. God is the God of reward, anything we do for Him. He is the One who brings everything in fulfillment.

To Stay Strong:

Fear does not have a place in our minds; we must remember we have the mind of Christ. We must praise the Lord for all the good things He has done for us.

When we decided to follow Jesus, and we have a great commitment to the presence of God. We must act on the Word of God to trust and to have peace in Him. We do not allow any doubt or fear near to us. We come against all demonic activities and cover ourselves by the blood of Jesus.

To continue walking in the holiness of God, it required obedience and making our faith strong. Then we acknowledge that we are sanctified and holy. We are living in the righteousness of God. No weapon forms against us shall prosper; the Fire of God will consume the devil's attack.

We decree the devil's plan shall be demolished, and we are living under the protection of the Lord. Let's plead the blood of Jesus over ourselves, our families, and our ministry.

Called to Preach:
If the Lord calls you to preach the Word of God, be willing to do anything in any place. Start to serve in a small area in the Kingdom of God. The Lord will confirm your call to preach. He will anoint you with the Holy Spirit.

We pray, sometimes we feel there are no open doors for us. But we are preparing ourselves for open doors opportunities that will lead us into the ministry. Reading the Word and decree the promise of God for what He has given us. We must remember what He has told us to do great work, and He shall fulfill His plan through us.

He will bring all His promise to pass; it might take time to be fulfilled. Sometimes we don't see any prayer has been answered. Or if we don't understand, but God is working to prepare something good for us. We shall always believe and trust Him that He hears our prayers. He will do everything in perfect time.

A few encouraging words to help us focus on Him:

- Do not lose your excitement to minister.
- Do not lose your joy in the Lord.
- Don't have any doubt in His Word.
- Don't get weary.
- Do not get angry with God.
- Do not get discouraged.
- Do not lose hope.
- Do not lose faith.

These words of encouragement will stir our spirits.
- Read and believe the Word.
- Decree His promise.
- Remind Him for His promise.
- Rejoice in the salvation of the Lord.
- Serve with excitement.
- Pray in the spirit.
- Pray for miracles and healing.
- Encourage yourself in the Word.
- Recognize the Word is only Hope.
- Being passionate to serve.

I want to share about how the Fire will come over us, how the Fire lives in us. How can we know we have the Fire of God? These questions would be asked many times.

I mentioned, the Fire is the Holy Spirit and the presence of God. The time, we accept Jesus as our personal Savior, we invite Him into our hearts. He comes in our lives by the Holy Spirit. Then we get a baptism in the Holy Spirit to receive the empowerment of the Spirit to become a witness to lost souls for the Lord Jesus.

Preaching with Boldness:

I believe, my preaching started with my praying in the spirit to release the anointing, then I began to preach boldly by the authority of God. The Fire came on me in my prayers. Since when I was young in the Lord, I pray with a loud voice. I always wanted to pray with boldness.

I am still praying loud and boldly. Maybe this just me, but I think God has made me pray boldly. But it also depends on having a strong personality that helps to become confident in the Lord. I love to preach powerfully, to encourage and to inspire more Christian believers from diverse denominations.

The Lord loves to watch us as we are serving Him in the spirit of dynamic, to preach with the Fire. He wants us to do our best in His Kingdom. He wishes us to seek Him, to depend on Him, and to stand on His Word.

We live on fire to make an effective prayer to decree the promise of God a little bit loud. God has not called us to be afraid or to be a shy person in public. I remember what the Holy Spirit reveals to me if I pray aloud and praying in the Spirit.

Actually, when I pray, I preach loud in the air and teach the Word to people around me and preaching to myself also. So, I go ahead and pray boldly and loud to hear myself. The devil will not like it. But the Holy Spirit is leading me into a dream and vision for my future ministry.

Preaching with Passion:
We recognize the Fire comes into our spirit. We must allow our passion to grow into a spiritual walk in the authority of the Lord. Our spiritual eyes will be open more to the things of God.

Allowing the fire burns in our souls, the good things the Fire will rise up in us. The only bad thing if we keep the Fire away from us by our own choices. We preach with no fire with empty words come out of us.

The Fire will burn in us wherever we go, and we carry His Word to preach. We can be a light into the darkness of the place where we walked in. We are living by faith and praising His name anywhere we enter in, we represent His Glory.

The Holy Spirit would love to reveal Jesus to us. He will make us like Jesus from Glory to Glory.

If we walk in the flesh, we have no passion for preaching. Then we will be serving and preaching without the anointing of God. Asking more of His anointing will give us new wisdom and knowledge of the Word of God.

1. A passionate preacher is dedicated to stand up and get ready to pray. To accomplish the impossible task of the Kingdom of God.
2. A passionate preacher is doing hard work to pray for the sake of others. To be enthusiastic about interceding for saving and healing others.
3. A passionate preacher is focused on the direction and the plan of God. It is needed to pray by the supernatural leadership of the Holy Spirit: seeing visions and dreams.
4. A passionate preacher is willing to go extra miles for others, ministering other believers and nonbelievers, and laying down his life in serving.

Defeat the Discouragement:
We need to ignore our negative thoughts and feelings. We have confidence that He continues to answer our prayer one at the time. It is a natural response to get discouraged by what we want from the Lord.

The Word of God can defeat discouragement for us. We're also claiming the devil is a liar and boldly proclaiming God's name. Jesus is in control of every prayer. The joy of Lord shall be our strength in good times and bad times. When we are in sad times in which we don't know what to do.

Sometimes we don't know what direction to take or what choice to make? But the joy of the Lord is always giving us power in trouble. To think positively about how the Lord is there for us and restores our faith. We must declare He is there, and let's encourages ourselves as King David encouraged himself to move forward.

Discouragement can paralyze us in rising up in spiritual life in Christ. It mainly will not allow us to grow in prayer life. Believing the Lord is ordering our step in His plan. Don't let discouragement to put you down or ruin your joy. Try hard and push forward.

"What then shall we say to these things? If God is for us, who can be against us?" Romans 8:31, NKJV.

• CHAPTER 15 •

How to become a Christian?

A CHRISTIAN WHO IS a follower of Jesus and trusts in him. The Bible gives a simple explanation so we can have a relationship with Him. We will have a spiritual experience as we become a born-again Christian believer.

The great news of the Christian doctrine appears with the concept that God has chosen us. He who formed us and created us in the image of His Son on this earth. I want just to take this opportunity to share about how we can have a personal relationship with Jesus by faith.

It is essential to follow the way of God's Word is better than doing any other ritual of Christianity. It will not help us become a Christian believer. When we recognize that we have sinned against God, and our sin will separate us from God, and it will lead us to death. We cannot make ourselves clean or forgive our own sins.

He came to die on the cross for our iniquities; he sacrificed his life. He shed His blood for our sins and sickness. Now we can go to Him by faith with no condemnation and no judgment. Becoming a Christian is to have a simple faith in the Lord, learning His Word, allowing ourselves to have a fellowship with other Christian believers in the church.

Then we build up our confidence in the Word and living more in the peace of Christ. We grow into a better spiritual maturity in walking with the Lord. When we move forward in faith, we develop our confidence in the Word of God only.

Let's focus on this part that we "believe" that Jesus is the Son of God. We are the sinners; we all need a Savior. He is the One who can save us from our sins. Now we repent our sins and accept Jesus into our hearts.

It is very simple to believe Jesus by faith. I will describe the few steps to remind us to make peace with our Heavenly Father, who loves us.

1. Believing in One true God and His Word
2. Repenting your sins
3. Inviting Jesus to come into your heart
4. Accepting Jesus as your Savior and Lord
5. To get baptized in water
6. Finding a Christian Fellowship to attend
7. Growing in the Spiritual life every day

When you follow these simple steps, you become a born-again Christian believer and welcome into God's family. When you are devoting your time in His presence and studying the Word of God, then the Holy Spirit reveals Jesus to you.

I am thrilled that you make the right decision to accept Jesus as your Savior. According to the Bible, you are saved, and He will forgive all your sins and wipe out your tears and restore you from all your iniquity.

Then, remember your name is written in the Book of Life in heaven. I want to lead you a short prayer of salvation.

Repeat after me:

Heavenly Father, I thank you for your Son Jesus; you sent Him to die on the cross for me in my place. He rose again, and He is alive again.

I repent from all my sins; I invite Jesus to come into my heart; I believe Jesus as my Lord and my Savior. Thank you for caring for me and accepting me as a child of God. In Jesus' name. Amen.

Conclusion

I WILL CONCLUDE THIS book by allowing me to serve you from my experience in the ministry. We learned from many beautiful stories in the Bible and how to declare a new life in a dark spirit. May we all apply the Word of God in our own personal walk with the Lord Jesus?

I am fired up that to have this opportunity to go through outline each chapter to bring an uplifting message of encouragement. We will discover that God can still fill us with His Fire, then we preach the Word with no fear. It was a delight to give you a demonstration of the presence of God.

We should all Christian keep the fire of the Holy Spirit burning. I love to stir every ministry, every preacher, and every ordinary servant of God, into outstanding humble leaders. Staying on fire for the Lord by decreeing the Glory come down!

He instructed us to focus on the important miracles of the Holy Spirit. Because of Him that we may turn into a powerful preacher. Therefore, let's have a passion for witnessing from home to the churches, from work to everywhere to share the Word of God.

He prepared the Kingdom of God for us that we can encounter His Glory. We carry His presence to present the message of salvation, healing, miracles, and hope to the world.

These powerful stories from the Old Testament would teach us to study the triumph of the Lord. As we know, the presence of God is the Fire of God was there to manifest God's Glory. As we understand, speaking and hearing the Word would build up our faith. It brings an enormous conviction for every person who wishes to live on the Fire.

This book will help you, energize you, and inspire you to turn into a mighty man or woman of God. I cherish to explore incredible stories about the Kingdom of God. I shared my own personal life would inspire you to stay focus and effective in this life.

May this book bless you and strengthen you in the Lord. I dream that this book will reach millions of Christian believers around the world. Thank you for supporting me, and it was my privilege to motivate you through this book, and may God bless you.

In the end, I would like to present my other books to you:
- Parables of Jesus
- Healing Miracles of Jesus
- Manifestation of Prayer
- Encouraging Stories in the Bible
- Authority in the Bible

About the Author

DR. DANIEL KAZEMIAN HAS dedicated his life to the nonprofit organization International Evangelistic Ministry, to preach the Good News by the anointing of the Holy Spirit. In June 1993, he was ordained to the ministry in the National Church of God by Dr. T. L. Lowery in Washington, DC.

He has since become one of today's most dynamic charismatic preachers. Christ walked into his life in January 1985, and Daniel was transformed into an exciting, enthusiastic dynamo for God. He's passionate about sharing God's love and saving grace with everyone, as well as healing the sick.

Daniel started his evangelistic career and his radio/TV ministry in Denmark-Scandinavia and abroad. He is now serving in the prophetic and healing ministry, and he ministers in churches, seminars, conventions, crusades, and anywhere the Spirit of God leads him.

Daniel earned his associate degree from the National Bible College and Seminary in June 1993 in Fort Washington, Maryland, and a bachelor's degree, a master's degree, and a Doctor of Theology degree from the International Theological Seminary in July 1996 in Plymouth, Florida.

He is the president of the nonprofit organization, International Evangelistic Ministry, located in Gainesville, Georgia.

Contact him through email: ieministry@hotmail.com

Visit our website: www.InternationalEvangelisticMinistry.com

www.ingramcontent.com/pod-product-compliance
Lightning Source LLC
Chambersburg PA
CBHW060823050426
42453CB00008B/565